The Believer's Daily Renewal

The Believer's Daily Renewal

Andrew Murray

 Bethany Fellowship INC.
MINNEAPOLIS, MINNESOTA 55438

Originally published in 1905 under the title *The Inner Chamber and the Inner Life*

Copyright © 1981
Bethany Fellowship, Inc.
All rights reserved

Published by Bethany Fellowship, Inc.
6820 Auto Club Road, Minneapolis, Minnesota 55438

Printed in the United States of America

Library of Congress Cataloging in Publication Data

Murray, Andrew, 1828-1917.
   The believer's daily renewal.

   1. Devotional calendars.   I. Title.
BV4811.M795   1981   248'.3   81-6143
ISBN 0-87123-147-6 (pbk.)   AACR2

About the Author

ANDREW MURRAY was born in South Africa in 1828. After receiving his education in Scotland and Holland, he returned to that land and spent many years there as both pastor and missionary. He was a staunch advocate of biblical Christianity. He is best known for his devotional books.

Preface

"Daily Renewal" suggests thoughts of the utmost importance. The daily need of solitude and quiet; the true spirit of prayer; the devotional reading of God's Word; the fellowship with God for which these are meant and by which alone they bring a blessing; the spiritual life which they are meant to strengthen and fit for duty in daily interaction with the world; the service for the Kingdom of God in soul-winning and intercession. All of these truths share in making our devotions a source of joy and strength. In this book I have not attempted to take them up systematically, but I hope that the fragments I have given may bring help to some as they cultivate the hidden life and its communion with God.

In my country there are various diseases that affect our orange trees. One of them is popularly known as "the root disease." A tree may still be bearing, and an ordinary observer may not notice anything wrong, yet an expert sees the beginning of a slow death.

The phylloxera in the vineyards is nothing but a root disease, and there is no radical cure but to take out the old roots and provide new ones. The original variety of grape is grafted on an American root, and in the course of time you have the same stem and branches and fruit as before—but the roots are new and able to resist the disease. It is in the part of the plant that is hidden from sight that the disease comes and where healing must be sought.

The Church of Christ, and the spiritual life of thousands of its members, suffers from the root disease—the neglect of secret communion with God. The lack of secret prayer, the neglect of the maintenance of the hidden life "*rooted* in Christ," "*rooted* and grounded in love," explains the inability of Christians to resist the world, and to bring forth fruit abundantly. Nothing can change this but restoration—in the life of the believer—of the "inner chamber" to the place which Christ meant it to have. As Christians learn not to trust their own efforts, but to daily strike their roots deeper into Christ, and to make secret personal fellowship with God their chief care, true godliness will flourish. "If the root be holy, so are the branches." If the morning hour be holy to the Lord, the day with its duties will be so too. If the root is healthy, so are the branches.

I pray that God may bless this book to some of His children as they pursue the deeper and more fruitful life, the life hid with Christ in God.

Andrew Murray

Contents

CHAPTER ONE

The Morning Hour

"My voice shalt thou hear in the morning, O Lord; in the morning will I direct my prayer unto thee, and will look up" (Ps. 5:3).

"The Lord God . . . wakeneth morning by morning, he wakeneth mine ear to hear as the learned" (Isa. 50:4).

From the earliest ages God's servants have thought of the morning as the time specially suited for the worship of God. It is still regarded by all Christians both as a duty and a privilege to devote some portion of the beginning of the day to seeking seclusion and fellowship with God. Many Christians observe the "Morning Watch"; some speak of it as the "Quiet Hour"; others use the name of the "Still Hour" or the "Quiet Time." All these, whether they mean a whole hour, half an hour, or a quarter of an hour, unite with the Psalmist in saying, "My voice shalt thou hear in the morning, O Lord."

In speaking of the extreme importance of this daily time of quiet for prayer and meditation on God's Word, Mr. Mott has said:

"Next to receiving Christ as Savior, and claiming the baptism of the Holy Spirit, we know of no act attended with larger good to ourselves or others than the formation of an undiscourageable resolution to keep the watch, and spend the first half hour of the day alone with God." At first glance the statement appears too strong. The act of receiving Christ as Savior is one of such infinite consequences for eternity, and the act of claiming the Holy Spirit is one that works such a revolution in the Christian life, that such a simple thing as the firm determination to keep the morning watch hardly appears sufficiently important to be placed next to them.

If, however, we think how impossible it is to daily live out our life in Christ as our Savior from sin, or to maintain a walk in the leading and power of the Holy Spirit, without daily, close fellowship with God, we soon shall see the truth of the statement. It simply reflects the fixed determination that Christ shall have the whole life, that the Holy Spirit shall in everything be fully obeyed. The morning watch is the key to maintaining the surrender to Christ and the Holy Spirit.

Let us look first at what ought to be the *object* of the morning watch. The morning watch must not be regarded as an end in itself. It is not sufficient that it gives us a blessed time for prayer and Bible study, thus providing a certain measure of refreshment and help. It is rather a means to an end. And that end is to *secure the presence of Christ for the whole day.*

Personal devotion to a friend or a pursuit means that that friend or pursuit shall always hold their place in the heart, even when other engagements occupy one's attention. Personal devotion to Jesus means that we allow nothing to separate us from Him for a moment. To abide in Him and His love, to be kept by Him and His grace, to be doing His will and pleasing Him, cannot possibly be an intermittent thing to one who is truly devoted to Him. "I need Thee every hour"; "Moment by moment I am kept in His love"; these hymns are the language of life and truth. "In thy name shall they rejoice all the day"; "I the Lord do keep it; I will water it every moment"—these are words of divine power. The believer cannot stand for one moment without Christ. Personal devotion to Him refuses to be content with anything less than to abide always in His love and His will;

the true scriptural Christian life is nothing less. This is the importance and blessedness and true aim of the morning watch.

The clearer our objective is the better we shall be able to use the means of attaining it. Consider the morning watch now as the means to this great end: *I want to secure absolutely the presence of Christ all the day, to do nothing that can interfere with it. I feel at once that my success for the day will depend upon the clarity and the strength of the faith that seeks and finds and holds Him in the closet.* Meditation and prayer and the Word will always be used as subordinate and auxiliary to this; the link for the day between Christ and me must be renewed and firmly fastened in the morning hour.

At first it may appear as if the thought of the upcoming day, with all its possible cares, pleasures and temptations, may disturb the rest I have enjoyed in my quiet devotion. It is possible; but it will be no loss. True religion aims at having the character of Christ so formed in us that in our most common acts, His temper and disposition shall show themselves. The spirit and the will of Christ are meant to so possess us that, in our conversations with men, in our relaxation, in our business, it shall be second nature for us to act according to them. All this can be, because Christ himself, as the Living One, *lives in us.* Be not disturbed if at first the goal appears too high or difficult, and occupies too much of your time in the hour of private prayer. The time you give it will be richly rewarded. You will return to prayer and scripture with new purpose and new faith. As the morning watch begins to have its effect on the day, the day will react on its first half hour, and fellowship with Christ will have new meaning and new power.

It will particularly have its influence on the spirit in which you keep the morning watch. As the grandeur of the aim (unbroken fellowship with God through the day) and the true nature of the means to secure it (a definite conscious meeting with Christ and a securing His presence for the day) possesses us, it will be seen that the one essential thing is *wholehearted purpose*—the fixed determination, whatever effort or self-denial it may cost, to win the prize.

In study or on the athletic field every student knows the need of vigorous will and determined purpose if he is to succeed. Religion needs, and indeed deserves, not less but more of such intense devotion. If anything, surely the love of Christ needs the whole heart. It is this fixed determination, before everything, to secure Christ's presence that will overcome every temptation to be unfaithful or superficial in the keeping of our pledges. It will make the morning watch a mighty means of grace in strengthening character, and enabling us to say no to every call for self-indulgence. It will enable us, when we enter the inner chamber and shut the door, to be there with our whole heart, ready at once for our communion with Christ. And this determination, from the morning watch on, will become the keynote of our daily life.

In the world it is often said, "Great things are possible to any man who knows what he wills, and wills it with all his heart." The student who has made a personal devotion to Christ his watchword will find in the morning hour the place where day by day the insight into his holy calling is renewed; where his will is braced up to walk worthy of it; and his faith is rewarded by the presence of Christ who waits to meet him and take charge of him for the day. We are more than conquerors through Him who loves us. A living Christ waits to meet us.

CHAPTER TWO

The Door Shut—Alone with God

> "When thou prayest enter into thy closet, and when thou hast shut thy door, pray to thy Father which is in secret" (Matt. 6:6).

Man was created for fellowship with God. God made him in His own image and likeness that he might be capable of understanding and enjoying God, entering into His will and delighting in His glory. Because God is the Everywhere-present and All-pervading One, man could have lived in an unbroken fellowship amidst whatever work he had to do.

Sin robbed us of this fellowship.

Nothing but this fellowship can satisfy the heart of either man or God. It was this Christ came to restore; to bring back to God His lost creature, and bring back man to all he was created for. Intimacy with God is the consummation of all blessedness on earth as in heaven. It comes when the promise, so often given, becomes a full experience—I will be with thee, I will never leave thee or forsake thee—when we can say, "The Father is always with me."

This communion with God is meant to be ours all the day, whatever our condition or the circumstances that surround us. But its enjoyment depends upon the reality of the fellowship in the inner chamber. The power to maintain close and glad fellowship with God all the day will depend entirely upon the intensity with which we seek to secure it in the hour of secret prayer. The one essential thing in the Morning Watch or the Quiet Hour is *fellowship with God.*

Our Lord teaches that this is to be the inner secret of secret prayer: "Shut thy door, pray to thy Father which is *in secret.*" The first and chief thing is to see that there in secret you have the Father's presence and attention. Know that He sees and hears you. Of more importance than all your earnestness and effort to pray aright is this one thing: the childlike, living assurance that your Father sees you, that you have now met Him, and that with His eye on you and yours on Him, you are now enjoying actual communion with Him.

Christian, there is a terrible danger to which you stand exposed in your inner chamber. You are in danger of substituting prayer and Bible study for living fellowship with God—the living interchange of giving Him your love, your heart, and your life, and receiving from Him His love, His life, and His spirit. Your needs and their expression, your desire to pray humbly and earnestly and believingly, may so occupy you that the light of His countenance and the joy of His love cannot enter you. Your Bible study may so interest you, and so waken pleasing religious sentiment, that the very Word of God may become a substitute for God himself; this is the greatest hindrance to fellowship because it keeps the soul occupied instead of leading it to God himself. Therefore we go out into the day's work without the power of an abiding fellowship, because in our morning devotions the blessing was not secured.

What a difference it would make in the life of many if everything in the closet were subordinate to this one thing: I want through the day to walk with God; my morning hour is the time when my Father enters into a definite agreement with me and I with Him that it shall be so. What strength would be imparted by the consciousness that God has taken charge of me, He himself is going with me; I am going to do

His will all day in His strength; I am ready for all that may come. What nobility would come into life if secret prayer were not only an asking for some new sense of comfort, or light, or strength, but also the surrendering of life just for one day into the sure and safe keeping of a mighty and faithful God.

"Pray to thy Father which is in secret; and thy Father which seeth in secret shall reward thee openly." When secret fellowship with the Father in spirit and in truth is maintained, the public life before men will manifest the reward. The Father who sees in secret takes charge and rewards openly. Separation from men, in solitude with God—this is the sure, the only way to associate with men in the power of God's blessing.

CHAPTER THREE

The Open Door—The Open Reward

"When thou fastest, anoint thine head and, wash thy face; that thou appear not unto men to fast, but unto thy Father which is in secret: and thy Father, which seeth in secret, shall reward thee openly" (Matt. 6:17, 18).

"When they saw the boldness of Peter and John . . . they took knowledge of them, that they had been with Jesus" (Acts 4:13).

"And it came to pass, when Moses came down from mount Sinai . . . that Moses wist not that the skin of his face shone while he talked with him. And when Aaron and all the children of Israel saw Moses, behold, the skin of his face shone; and they were afraid to come nigh him. And till Moses had done speaking with them, he put a veil on his face" (Ex. 34:29, 30, 33).

The transition from the fellowship with God in the morning hour to the interaction with our fellowmen is often difficult. If we have met God, we long to maintain the sense of His presence and our surrender to Him. We go out to the breakfast table, where, perhaps in the bosom of our own family, the atmosphere is suddenly changed, and as the presence of men and the visible asserts itself, we begin to lose what we have found. Many a young Christian has been perplexed with the question of how to keep his heart filled with that which he does not feel at liberty, or has not the opportunity, to discuss. Even in religious circles it is not al-

ways easy to have free conversation, through lack of fervor
or boldness, about that which would give the greatest profit
and pleasure. Let us strive to learn how our relations with
men may be, instead of a hindrance, a help to the maintenance of a life in continual fellowship with God.

The lessons which the story of Moses with the veil on his
face teach are vivid. Close and continued fellowship with
God will, in due time, leave its mark and make itself manifest to men. Moses was unaware that his face shone; the
light of God shining from us will be unconscious, but it will
deepen our sense of being an earthen vessel (1 Cor. 2:3, 4;
2 Cor. 4). The sense of God's presence in a man may often
cause others to fear, or at least to feel ill at ease in, his com-
pany. When others observe what is in him, the true believer
will know what it is to veil his face, and prove by humility
and love that he is indeed a man of like passions with those
around him. And yet, there will be the proof, too, that he is
a man of God who lives in, and has dealings with, an unseen
world.

The same lessons are taught by what our Lord says
about fasting. Make no show of your fasting, so that you appear to men not to fast; meet them in the joy and kindness
of God's gentleness, as the Father's beloved and loving
child. Count upon God, who has seen you in secret, to reward you openly, to give you grace, as you deal with men, to
maintain your communion with Him, and to make them
know that His grace and light are on you.

The story of Peter and John confirms the same truth:
they had been with Jesus not only while He was on earth,
but also as He entered into the heavenlies, and they had received His spirit. They simply acted out what the spirit of
Christ taught them; even enemies could see by their boldness that they had been with Jesus.

The blessing of communion with God may easily be lost
by entering too deeply into fellowhip with men. The spirit
of the inner chamber must be sustained by a holy watchful-

ness throughout the day—we know not at what hour the enemy may come. This continuance of the morning watch may be maintained by a quiet self-restraint in not giving the reins to nature. It has, in a religious home circle, often received help, as each one repeats a text at the breakfast table on some fixed subject, giving easy occasion to spiritual conversation. Once the abiding sense of God's presence and of communion with Him—"be thou in the fear of God all the day long"—has become the aim of the morning hour as well as deep humility and loving relationship with those around us, grace will be sought and found to proceed into the day's duties with unbroken continuity of fellowship. It is a great thing to enter the inner chamber, to shut the door, and meet the Father in secret. It is a greater thing to open the door again and go out, enjoying that presence which nothing can disturb.

To some, such a life does not appear necessary; the strain is too great—one can be a good Christian without it. To those who seek to be men of one purpose, who feel that to mightily influence the church and the world around them they must be full of God and His presence, everything will be subordinate to one issue: how to bear in the earthen vessel the heavenly treasure—the power of Christ resting on us all the day.

CHAPTER FOUR

Moses and the Word of God

In regard to the connection between prayer and the Word in our private devotion, the expression of a convert from heathenism has often been quoted: "I pray, I speak to God; I read in the Bible, God speaks to me." There is a verse in the history of Moses, in which this thought is beautifully illustrated. We read, "When Moses was gone into the tabernacle . . . to speak with [God], then he heard the voice of one speaking unto him from off the mercy seat . . . and [God] spake unto him" (Num. 7:89). When he went in to pray for himself or his people, and to wait for instructions, Moses found One waiting for him. What a lesson for our morning watch. A prayerful spirit is the spirit to which God will speak. A prayerful spirit will be a listening spirit waiting to hear what God says. In my communion with God, His presence and the part He takes must be as real as my own.

What is needed that our Scripture reading and praying may be such true fellowship with God? First, *get into the right place.* Moses went into the tabernacle to speak with God. He separated himself from the people, and went where he could be alone with God. He went to the place where God was to be found. Jesus has told us where that place is. He calls us to enter into our closet, shut the door, and pray to our Father "which seeth in secret." Anyplace where we really are alone with God may be to us the secret of His presence. Speaking with God requires separation from all else. It needs a heart intently set upon and in full expectation of meeting God personally, and having direct dealings with Him. Those who go there to speak to God will hear the "voice of one speaking" to them.

Next, *get into the right position.* He heard the "voice of one speaking . . . from off the mercy seat." *Bow* before the mercy seat. There the consciousness of your unworthiness will not hinder you but be a real help in trusting God. There you may have the assured confidence that your upward look will be met by His eye, that your prayer can be heard, that His loving answer will be given. Bow before the mercy seat, and be sure that the God of Mercy will see and bless you.

Finally, *get into the right disposition*—the listening attitude. Many are so occupied with the much or the little they have to say in their prayers that the "voice of one" speaking off the mercy seat is never heard because it is not expected or waited for. "Thus saith the Lord, The heaven is my throne, and the earth is my footstool. . . . To this man will I look, even to him that is poor and of a contrite spirit, and trembleth at my word" (Isa. 66:1).

Let us enter the closet and set ourselves to pray with a heart that humbly waits to hear God speak; in the Word we read we shall indeed hear the "voice of one speaking" to us. The highest blessing of prayer will come as we cease to pray and let God speak.

Prayer and the Word are inseparably linked together; power in the use of either depends upon the presence of the other. The Word gives me the subject for prayer, telling me what God will do for me. It shows me the path of prayer, telling me how God would have me come. It gives me the power for prayer—courage from the assurance I will be heard. And it brings me the answer to prayer as it teaches what God will do for me. On the other hand, prayer prepares the heart for receiving the Word from God himself, for receiving the spiritual understanding from the Spirit, for building faith that participates in its mighty working.

It is clear why this is so. Prayer and the Word have one

common center—God. Prayer seeks God; the Word reveals God. In prayer man asks God; in the Word God answers man. In prayer man rises to heaven to dwell with God; in the Word God comes to dwell with man. In prayer man gives himself to God; in the Word God gives himself to man.

In prayer and the Word God must be all. Make God the all of your heart, the one object of your desire; prayer and the Word will be a blessed fellowship with God, the interchange of thought, and love and life—dwelling in God and God in us. Seek God and live!

CHAPTER FIVE

Moses the Man of Prayer

Preceding Moses was the patriarchal dispensation, marked by the family life and the power the fathers had. Moses is the first man appointed to be a teacher and leader of men. In him we find wonderful illustrations of the place and power of intercession in the life of the servant of God.

In Egypt, from his first call, Moses prayed. He asked God what he was to say to the people (Ex. 3:11-13). He told God of all his weakness, and begged Him to be relieved of his mission (4:1-13). When the people reproached him because their workload was increased, he went and told God (5:22), and expressed to Him all his fears (6:12). This was his first training. Out of this was born his power in prayer when, time after time, Pharaoh asked him to entreat the Lord for him, and deliverance came at Moses' request (8:8, 9, 12, 28, 29, 30, 31; 9:28, 29, 33; 10:17, 18). Study these passages until you come under the full impression of how real a factor prayer was in Moses' work and God's redemption.

At the Red Sea, Moses cried to God with the people and the answer came (14:15). In the wilderness when the people thirsted, and when Amalek attacked them, it was also prayer that brought deliverance (17:4, 11).

At Sinai, when Israel had made the golden calf, it was prayer that immediately averted the threatened destruction (32:11, 14). It was renewed prayer that gained them restoration (32:31). It was more prayer that secured God's presence to go with them (33:17), and once again it was prayer that brought the revelation of God's glory (33:19). And when that had been given it was fresh prayer that received the renewal of the covenant (34:9,10).

In Deuteronomy we have a wonderful summary of all this (9:18, 19, 20, 26); we see with what intensity Moses prayed, and how in one case he fell on his face before the Lord for forty days and forty nights (9:25; 10:10).

In Numbers we read of Moses' prayer quenching the fire of the Lord (11:2), and obtaining the supply of meat (11:11, 18); of prayer healing Miriam (12:13); of prayer again saving the nation when they had refused to go up to the land (14:17-20). Prayer brought down judgment on Korah (16:15), and when God would consume the whole congregation, prayer made atonement (v. 46). Prayer brought water out of the rock (20:6), and in answer to prayer the brazen serpent was given (21:7). Through prayer God's will was discerned in a difficult case (27:5) and Joshua was named as Moses' successor (v. 16).

Study all this until your heart is filled with the thought of the role prayer must play in the life of a man who would be God's servant to his fellowmen.

As we study, the parts will unite into a living whole and Moses will become a living model for our prayer life. We shall learn what is needed to be an intercessor. The lessons that will come to us will be such as these:

1. Moses was devoted to God, zealous, even jealous for God, for His honor and will.

2. Moses was devoted to his people, ready to sacrifice himself if they could be saved.

3. Moses was conscious of a divine calling to act as mediator, to be the channel of communication and of blessing, between a God in heaven and men on earth. A life can be so entirely possessed by this mediatorial consciousness that nothing is more simple and natural than to expect that God will hear.

4. God, in answer to the prayers of one man, saves and blesses those entrusted to the man, and does what He would not do without those prayers. The whole government of God has included prayer in its plan as one of its constituent parts. Heaven is filled with the life and power and

blessing earth needs, and the prayer of earth is the power to bring that blessing down.

5. Prayer is an index of the spiritual life, and its power depends upon my relation to God, and my consciousness of being His representative. He entrusts His work to me, and the more simple and entire my devotion to His interests is, the more natural and certain the assurance that He hears me becomes.

Think of the position God had in Moses' life; He was the God who had sent him, the God to whom he was wholly devoted, the God who had promised to be with him, and who would always help him when he prayed.

How do we learn to pray like Moses? We cannot secure this grace by an act of the will. Our first lesson must be the sense of impotence. Then grace will work it in us, slowly and surely, if we give ourselves to its training. Though the training will be gradual, one thing can be done immediately: we can *at once* decide to give ourselves to this life and take up the right position. Make the decision now to live only to be a channel for God's blessing to flow to the world. Take the step. If need be, take ten minutes for deliberate thought. Accept the divine appointment, and take up some object of intercession.

Take time, say a week, and get firm hold of the elementary truths Moses' example teaches. As a music teacher insists upon practicing the scales—only practice makes perfect—set yourself to learn thoroughly and to apply the needed first lessons.

God seeks men through whom He can bless the world. Say, "Here am I; I will give my life to this." Cultivate large faith in the simple truth: *God hears prayer; God will do what I ask.*

Give yourself as wholly to men as you have to God, and open your eyes to the need of a perishing world. Take up your *position* in Christ, and in the *power* which His name, and life and Spirit give you. And begin to practice definite intercession.

CHAPTER SIX

Moses the Man of God

"Moses the man of God blessed the children of Israel"
(Deut. 33:1).

The man of God. How much the name means! It describes a man who comes from God, chosen and sent by Him; a man who walks with God, lives in His fellowship and carries the mark of His presence; a man who lives for God and His will, whose being is pervaded and ruled by the glory of God, who involuntarily and unceasingly causes men to think of God; a man in whose heart God has taken the rightful place as the All in All, who only desires that God should have that place throughout the world.

Such men of God are what the world needs; such men are what God seeks, that He may fill them with himself and send them out to help others to know Him. Moses was such a man; men naturally spoke of him as Moses the man of God! Every servant of God should aim at being such a person—a living witness and proof of what God is to him in heaven, and on earth, and what He claims to be.

In a previous chapter we spoke of communion with God as man's purpose, as the privilege of daily life, as the primary concern in the morning watch. This chiefly referred to our personal need and to the power of a godly, happy life that can influence others. The term, Moses the man of God, and the thought of Moses being so closely and manifestly linked to God that this was his chief characteristic, leads us farther. It leads us out into public life, suggesting that the

impression we can make upon men, and the power we can
have as we manifest God's presence will cause men to auto-
matically think of us as "the man of God!"

These are the men the world and God equally need. And
why? Because the world, by sin, has fallen away from God.
Because in Christ the world has been redeemed for God.
Because God cannot show men what they ought to be, and
awaken, call, and help them, except through men of God, in
whom His life, spirit, and power are working. Man was
created for God that God might live, work, and display His
glory in him and through him. God intends to be his all in
all. The indwelling of God should be as natural and delight-
ful as it is true and incomprehensible. When the redemption of Christ was completed by the descent of the Holy
Spirit into the hearts of men, this indwelling was restored;
God regained possession of His home. And where a man
surrenders himself wholly to the presence of the Holy Spirit, not only as a power working in him, but as God dwelling
in him (John 14:16, 20, 23; 1 John 4), he may become, in the
fullest meaning of the word, a man of God!

Paul tells us that through the power of Holy Scripture
"the man of God may be perfect." This suggests that with
some the life is imperfect, and needs to be made perfect.
"All scripture is given by the inspiration of God, and is
profitable for doctrine, for reproof, for correction, for instruction in righteousness: that the man of God may be perfect, throughly furnished unto all good works" (2 Tim.
3:16, 17). This brings us to the morning watch as the chief
time for personal Bible study. As we yield heart and life to
the Word's teaching, reproof, correction, and instruction
that expose and mold our whole life, we come under the direct influence of God, and into full communion with Him
"that the man of God may be perfect, throughly furnished
unto all good works."

Oh, for grace to be truly a man of God! A man that
knows and proves these three things: God *is* all, God *claims*

all, God *works* all; a man that sees God's place in His universe and in men—the All in all; a man who understands that God demands and must have all, who only lives to give God His due glory; a man who seeks, like the Son of God, to live in unceasing blessed dependence on the Father in Him who speaks the words and does the work.

Seek to be a man of God! Let God, in the morning watch and during the day, be all to you. Let your life be devoted to one thing: to bring men to God and God to men, so that in His Church and in the world, God may have His rightful place.

"If I be a man of God, then let fire come down from heaven" (2 Kings 1:10), Elijah answered when the captain ordered him to come down. The true God answers by fire. And the true man of God knows how to call down the fire because he has power with the God of heaven. Whether the fire be judgment or the Holy Spirit, the man of God's task is to bring fire down to earth. The world needs the man of God who knows God's power, and his power with God.

It is in the secret prayer habit of daily life that we learn to know our God and His fire, and our power with Him. Know what it is to be a man of God, and what it implies! In Elijah as in Moses it means a separation from every other interest, an entire identification with the honor of God, no longer a man of the world, but *a man of God*.

There is a secret feeling that all this brings more strain and sacrifice, difficulty and danger, than we are ready for. This is true only if we have not seen how absolute God's claim is, how blessed it is to yield to it, and how certainly God himself will work it in us.

Turn back now and look at Moses the man of prayer, Moses the man of the Word; see how these produced *Moses the man of God*. See the same in the life of Elijah—the harmony between our hearing God's word and His hearing ours; it becomes divinely possible to be and live as *a man of God*.

CHAPTER SEVEN

The Power of God's Word

"The word of God which effectually worketh also in you that believe" (1 Thess. 2:13).

The value of a man's words depends upon my knowledge of him. What a difference between the words of men who promise, "I will give you half of all I have," if one is a poor man, and the other is a millionaire. Therefore, one of the first requisites to fruitful Bible study is the knowledge of God the Omnipotent One, and of the power of His Word.

The power of God's word is infinite. "By the word of the Lord were the heavens made. . . . For he spake and it was done; he commanded and it stood fast" (Ps. 33:6, 9). God's omnipotence works in His Word; it has creative power and calls into existence the very thing of which it speaks.

The Word of the living God is a living word and gives life. It cannot only call into existence, but even make alive that which is dead; its power can raise dead bodies and give eternal life to dead souls. All spiritual life comes through it, for we are born of incorruptible seed by the Word of God that lives and abides forever.

Here is one of the deepest secrets of receiving the blessing of God's word: *faith* in its creative and quickening energy—*faith that the word will work in me the very thing which it commands or promises.* It "effectually worketh in you that believe." Nothing can resist its power when received into the heart through the Holy Spirit. "The voice of the Lord is in power." Everything depends upon learning the art of receiving this word into the heart. First, you must exercise *faith* in its living, omnipotent, creative power.

By His word God "calleth those things which be not as though they were" (Rom. 4:17). As this is true of all God's mighty deeds from creation to the resurrection of the dead, it is true also of every word in His holy book. Two things keep us from believing this as we should. The first is the terrible experience in the world around, and perhaps in ourselves, too, of the Word being made ineffectual by human wisdom, unbelief, or worldliness. The other is neglect of the teaching of Scripture that the word is a *seed*. Seeds are small, they may be long dormant, they have to be hidden, and once they sprout they grow slowly. Because the effect of God's Word is also hidden and unobserved, slow and apparently feeble, we do not believe in its omnipotence. Make this one of your first lessons: *The Word I study is the power of God unto salvation; it will work in me all I need, all the Father asks.*

What a prospect such faith would open up for our spiritual life! We would find all the treasures and blessings of God's grace within our reach. The Word has power to enlighten our darkness; in our hearts it will bring the light of God, the sense of His love, and the knowledge of His will. The Word can fill us with strength and courage to conquer every enemy, and to do whatever God asks us to do. The Word can cleanse, sanctify, develop faith and obedience, and become in us the seed of every character-trait of our Lord. Through the Word, the Spirit can lead us into all truth—make all that is in the Word true in us—and thus prepare our heart to be the habitation of the Father and the Son.

What a change would occur in your attitude toward God's Word and the morning watch if you really believed this simple truth. Begin training for that ministry of the Word, which every believer must exercise, by proving its power in your own experience. Begin to seek this, quietly setting yourself to learn the great faith-lesson, the mighty power of God's Word: The Word of God is true *because God himself will make it true in us!* You shall have much to learn, much to overcome, and much to surrender to see that power. But this will come true if you will only approach your Bible study determined to believe that God's Word has omnipotent power in your heart to work every blessing which it promises.

CHAPTER EIGHT

The Seed Is the Word

I think that in all nature there is no other illustration of the Word of God as true and full of meaning as that of the seed. To have full spiritual insight into it is a wonderful means of grace.

The points of resemblance are obvious. There is the apparent insignificance of the seed—a little thing as compared with the tree that springs from it. There is the life, enclosed and dormant within a husk. There is the need of suitable soil, without which growth is impossible. There is the slow growth, calling for the long patience of the husbandman. And there is the fruit, in which the seed reproduces and multiplies itself. In all these respects, the seed teaches us precious lessons about our use of God's Word.

First there is the lesson of FAITH. Faith does not look at appearances. By human judgment it looks most improbable that a word of God should give life in the soul, should work in us the very grace of which it speaks, should transform our whole character, should fill us with strength. And yet it does. Once we have learned to believe that the Word can effect the very truth which it expresses, we have found one of the chief secrets of Bible study. We can then receive each word as the pledge and the power of God's working in us.

Then there is the lesson of LABOR. The seed needs to be gathered, kept, and put into prepared soil. So also the mind has to gather from Scripture, understand and pass on to the

heart—the only soil in which this heavenly seed can grow—
the words which meet our need. We cannot give the life or
the growth, nor do we need to—it is there. But what we can
do is hide the word in our heart, waiting for the sunshine
that comes from above.

The seed also teaches the lesson of PATIENCE. The
Word's effect on the heart is, in most cases, not immediate.
It needs time to develop roots and grow up—Christ's words
must *abide* in us. We must not only increase our store of Bible knowledge daily—gather the grain in a barn—but
watch over those commands or promises that we have
claimed, and allow them room in our heart to spread both
root and branches. We need to know what seed we have put
in, and to cultivate a watchful but patient expectancy. In
due time we shall reap if we faint not.

Last comes the lesson of FRUITFULNESS. However in-
significant that little seed of a word of God appears, however feeble its life may seem, however deep its meaning
may be hidden, and however slow its growth may be, be
sure *the fruit will come.* The very truth, life, and power of
God, of which the word contained the thought, will grow
and ripen within you. Just as a seed produces fruit, contain-
ing the same seed for new reproduction, so the word will not
only bring you the fruit it promised, but that fruit will become seed which you carry to others to give life and blessing.

Not only the Word, but "the *kingdom of heaven* is like a
seed." And all the grace of it comes as a seed hidden in the
heart of the regenerate. Christ is a seed. The Holy Spirit is a
seed. The love of God shed abroad in the heart is a seed.
The "exceeding greatness of this power" that works in us is
a seed. The life is hidden there in the heart, but not instant-
ly or incessantly *felt* in its power. The divine glory is there,
but often without form or comeliness, to be known only by
faith, to be counted and acted on even when not felt, to be
waited for in its springing forth and its growth.

When this central truth is firmly held as the law of all the heavenly life on earth, the study of God's Word becomes an act of faith, surrender, and dependence upon the living God. I believe humbly in the divine seed that is in the Word. I believe in the power of God's Spirit to make the Word true in my experience. I yield my heart hungrily and wholly to receive this divine seed. And I wait on God in absolute dependence and confidence to give the increase with power beyond what I can ask or think.

CHAPTER NINE

Obedience and Knowledge

"But [Jesus] said, Yea rather, blessed are they that hear the word of God, and keep it" (Luke 11:28).

"If any man will do his will, he shall know" (John 7:17).

I once received a letter from an evidently earnest Christian, asking me for some hints to help him in Bible study. My first thought was that there are so many addresses and booklets on the subject that he would find all I could say better said already. However, certain experiences in my own immediate circle soon showed me the need for instruction on this all-important subject; I found there were points to which special emphasis should be given. I pray and hope that what I now write may be from God, the fountain of light and life, to help His young children draw from His precious Word all that divine instruction and nourishment, all that abundant joy and strength which He has laid up for them.

Here I address a young Christian who has said to me, "Help me to study my Bible. Give me some rules for how to begin, and how to go on, so that I may know my Bible well."

The thing that comes before all else is this: In your Bible study everything will depend upon *the spirit in which you approach it*—the objective you propose. In worldly things a man is ruled and urged on by the goal he sets before himself. It is no different with the Bible. If your aim be simply to know the Bible well, you will be disappointed. If you think that a thorough knowledge of the Bible will necessarily be a blessing, you are mistaken. To some it is a curse. To others it is powerless, not making them either holy or happy. To some it is a burden, depressing them instead of quickening or lifting them up.

What ought to be the real objective of the Bible student? God's Word is food, bread from heaven; the first need for Bible study is *a great hunger after righteousness*, a great desire to do all God's will. The Bible is a light; the first condition to its enjoyment is a hearty longing to walk in God's ways. Is not this what the texts I began with teach us? "Blessed are they that hear the word of God and keep it." The Word is nothing if it is not obeyed. "If any man will do his will, he shall know." All true knowledge of God's Word depends upon there being first the will to obey it. This is the very lesson we are enforcing. God will unlock the real meaning and blessing of His Word only to those whose will is definitely set upon obeying it. I must read my Bible with one purpose: "Whatsoever he saith unto you, do it."

This is easily understood when we think of what *words* are meant for. They stand between the will and the deed. A man wills to do something for you; before he does it, he expresses his thought or purpose in words; then he fulfills the words by doing what he has promised. So also with God. His words derive their value from what He does. In creation His word was with power; He spoke and it was done. In grace He does what He says. David prays (2 Sam. 7:25), "Do as thou hast said." Solomon says at the consecration of the temple: "Who hath with his hand fulfilled that which he spake with his mouth"; "[who] hath performed his word that he hath spoken"; "which hast kept . . . that which thou hast promised . . . and spake it with thy mouth, and hast fulfilled it with thine hand"; "let thy word be verified, which thou hast spoken" (2 Chron. 6:4, 10, 15, 17). Through the prophets, God says, "I the Lord have spoken it; *I will do it.*" And they reply, "What thou hast spoken, *is done.*" The truth and worth of God's promises consist in the fact that *He fulfills them.* His words of promise are meant to be fulfilled.

This is no less true of His commands, which He intends us to obey. If we do not obey them, if we seek to know them, and admire their beauty and praise their wisdom, but do not obey them, we delude ourselves. *They are meant to be obeyed;* as we obey them their real meaning and blessing can be revealed to us. Only as we obey can we really grow in the divine life. "Walk worthy of the Lord unto all pleasing, being fruitful in every good work [this first, then], and increasing in the knowledge of God" (Col. 1:10). Only when we approach God's words with the same object which God had in view—that they should be obeyed—can we have any hope of blessing.

We see this all around us in the pursuit of knowledge, or in any branch of trade. The apprentice or pupil is expected to put the lessons he receives into practice; only then is he prepared for further teaching. Even so in the Christian life, Bible study is mere theory, a pleasing exercise of mind and imagination, worth little or nothing for true holiness or Christlikeness until the student is ready never to open or close his Bible without making God's purpose His very own. He listens when God says, "Do all that I speak."

This was the mark of the saints of old. "Thus did Moses: according to all that the Lord commanded him, so did he" is the description of a man who, as a servant, was faithful in all his house. Of David we read, "I have found . . . a man after mine own heart, who shall fulfill all my will." In Psalm 119 we hear him speak with God about His Word, and pray for divine light and teaching, but always including the vow of obedience, or some other expression of love and delight. Obeying God's will, even for God's own Son, is the one secret of entrance into the favor and the mind of God.

I have just been reading Dwight L. Moody's book, *Pleasure and Profit in Bible Study.* I am certain many will use the suggestions it contains, thinking what has helped a man like Mr. Moody can help me, too. And yet they will be disappointed—*unless* they bring to the Bible what Mr. Moody brought: an honest desire to do whatever he saw God wanted him to do. Young Christian, "I beseech you by the mercies of God," when you ask God to lead you into the treasures of His Word, into the palace where Christ dwells, "present yourself as a living sacrifice," ready to do whatever God shall speak. Do not consider this a matter of course. It is of deeper importance than you know. This attitude is more frequently absent from Bible study than you think. Seek with deep humility. The first need for enjoying your food is hunger. The first requirement for the Bible study is a simple, determined longing to find out what God wants you to do, and a dead-in-earnest resolve to do it. "If any man will do his will"—the Word of God will be opened up to him.

CHAPTER TEN

The Blessedness of the "Doer"

> "Be ye doers of the word, and not hearers only, deceiving your own selves. But . . . being not a forgetful hearer but a doer of the word, this man shall be blessed in his deed" (James 1:22, 25).

What a terrible delusion to be contented and delighted in hearing the Word and yet not "doing" it. It is terribly common for multitudes of Christians to listen to the Word of God regularly and earnestly and yet not obey it. If their own employee were to do so—hearing but not doing—they would be furious. And yet, so complete is the delusion, they never realize that they are not living good Christian lives. What causes this delusion?

For one thing, people mistake the pleasure they have in hearing for spirituality and worship. The mind delights in having the truth clearly presented; the imagination is gratified by its illustration; the emotions are stirred by its application. To an active mind, knowledge gives pleasure. A man may study some branch of science—say electricity— for the enjoyment the knowledge gives him, without the least intention of applying it practically. And so people go to church and enjoy the preaching; yet they do not do what God asks. The unconverted and the converted man alike remain content to continue sinning, confessing, and sinning again.

Another cause of this delusion is the terrible perversion of the doctrine of our impotence to do good. The grace of Christ that can enable us to obey, keep us from sinning and make us holy, is rarely believed. Men practically think that the necessity of sinning infects them—God cannot expect exact obedience of them, for He knows they cannot render it. This error cuts away the very root of a person's determination to do all God has said. It closes the heart to any earnest desire to believe and experience all God's grace can do in us, and keeps men self-contented in the midst of sin. Hearing and not doing—what terrible self-delusion.

There is a third reason, with special reference to private Bible reading: the hearing or reading is regarded as a duty, a religious service. We have spent our five or ten minutes in the morning reading; we have read thoughtfully and attentively; we have tried to absorb what we read. Such a duty faithfully performed eases the conscience and gives a sense of satisfaction. Such an approach is not only worthless, but will have a hardening influence on the heart. We must set our whole heart upon literally doing and being what God's Word says. "Be ye doers of the word, and not hearers only, deceiving your own selves."

It is in the closet, in the morning watch, that this delusion must be fought and conquered. We may find that it will disturb our regular Bible reading and make us fall behind in our schedule. This need not happen, but far better it should than that this issue remain doubtful and unsettled. Everything depends on this. Our Lord Jesus said, "If any man will to do his will, he shall know of the doctrine, whether it be of God." Only the heart that delights in God's law, and has set its will to obey it, can receive the divine illumination, which spiritually knows the teaching of Christ in its divine origin and power. Without this will to obey, our knowledge will not profit; it is mere head knowledge.

In life, in science and art, in business, the only way of truly knowing is doing. What a man cannot do he does not thoroughly know. The only way to know God, to taste His blessedness, is through the doing of His will. That proves whether it is a God of my own sentiment and imagination that I confess, or the true and living God who rules all. Only by doing His will can I prove I love and accept it, and make myself one with it. And there is no possible way under heaven of being united to God but by being united to His will through doing it. The self-delusion of hearing and not doing is conquered in the quiet of the inner chamber, in the spirit in which I do my private Bible reading, in the determination to absolutely settle the issue of, "I am going to do whatever God says."

Here is how we should approach a portion of God's Word. Suppose it to be the Sermon on the Mount. I begin with the first Beatitude: "Blessed are the poor in spirit." I ask, "What does this mean? Am I obeying this injunction? Am I earnestly seeking, day by day, to maintain this disposition? Am I willing to wait, and plead with Christ, and believe that He can develop it in me? Am I going to *do* this—to be poor in spirit? Or shall I again be a hearer and not a doer?"

And so I may go through the Beatitudes, and through the whole Sermon, and verse by verse ask, "Do I know what this means? Am I living it out?" And as usual, the answer comes, "No. I see no possibility of living thus, and doing what He says." I shall feel the need of an entire revision of both my beliefs and behavior. And I shall wonder whether the vow "Whatever he says, I am going to do" has ever been a reality, either in my Bible reading or my life.

Such introspection may generate in me a poverty of spirit I have never experienced, give me entirely new insight into my need for a Christ who will breathe into me His own life, and accomplish in me all He speaks. I will gain courage in faith to say, " 'I can do all things through Christ which strengtheneth me.' Whatever He says in His Word, I will do."

CHAPTER ELEVEN

Keeping Christ's Commandments

"If ye know these things, happy are ye if you do them" (John 13:17).

The blessedness and the blessing of God's Word is only to be known by obeying it.

The subject is of such supreme importance in the Christian life, and therefore in our Bible study, that I return to it once more, this time considering the one expression, keeping the commandments.

Let us study it first in the "farewell discourse."

"If ye love me, keep my commandments. And . . . the Father . . . shall give you another Comforter" (John 14:15, 16).

"He that hath my commandments, and keepeth them, he it is that loveth me; and he . . . shall be loved of my Father" (14:21).

"If a man love me, he will keep my words; and my Father will love him" (14:23).

"If ye abide in me, and my words abide in you, ye shall ask what ye will, and it shall be done unto you" (15:7).

"If ye keep my commandments, ye shall abide in my love" (15:10).

"Ye are my friends, if ye do whatsoever I command you" (15:14).

Study and compare these passages until the words enter your heart and convince you that keeping Christ's commandments is the indispensable condition of all true spiritual blessing. This includes the coming of the Holy Spirit, His actual indwelling, the enjoyment of the Father's love, the inward manifestation of Christ, the abode of the Father and the Son in the heart, the power of prayer, the abiding in Christ's love, and the enjoyment of His friendship. The power to claim and enjoy these blessings in faith daily necessitates the childlike consciousness that we do keep His commandments. For fruitful Bible study, we must *expect* divine light and strength with every word of God, because He knows that we are ready to obey implicitly. Delighting in, and doing the will of God, is our only way to the heart of the Father, and His only way to our heart. Keep the commandments; this is the way to every blessing.

All this is strikingly confirmed by what we find in John's first epistle. "Hereby we do know that we know him, if we keep his commandments. He that saith, I know him, and keepeth not his commandments, is a liar. . . . But whoso keepeth his word, in him verily is the love of God perfected" (2:3-5). Keeping His Word is the only proof of true, saving knowledge of God, of not being self-deceived in our religion, of God's love being possessed, not imagination.

"If our heart condemn us not, then have we confidence toward God. And whatsoever we ask we receive of him, because we keep his commandments. . . . And he that keepeth his commandments, dwelleth in him" (3:21, 22, 24). Keeping the commandments is the secret of confidence toward God and intimate fellowship with Him.

"This is the love of God, that we keep his commandments. . . . For whatsoever is born of God overcometh the world" (5:3, 4). Our profession of love is worthless unless proven true by the keeping of His commandments in the power of a life born of God. Knowing God, having the love of God perfected in us, having boldness with God, abiding in Him, being born of Him and loving Him—all these depend on one thing: *keeping the commandments.*

When we realize the prominence Christ and Scripture give to this truth, we shall learn to give it the same prominence in our life. It will become one of the keys to true Bible study. The person who reads his Bible, with longing and determination to find and to obey every commandment of God and of Christ, is on the right track to receiving all the blessing the Word was ever meant to bring. He will especially learn two things: the need to wait for the Holy Spirit to lead him into all God's will, and the blessedness of performing daily duties, not only because they are right, or he delights in them, but because they are the will of God. He will find how all daily life is elevated when he says as Christ did, "This commandment have I received of my Father." The Word will become the light and guide by which all his steps are ordered. His life will become a training school in which the sanctifying power of the Word is proved, and his mind will continually receive its teaching and encouragement. Thus, the keeping of the commandments will be the key to every spiritual blessing.

Make a determined effort to grasp what this life of full obedience means. Take some of Christ's clearest commands—"Love one another; as I have loved you"; "ye also ought to wash one another's feet"; "ye should do as I have done to you"—and practice Christlike love and humility as the law of the supernatural life you are to live.

When the sense of failure or impotence tempt you to despair or to rest contented in what you think attainable, let it only encourage you to put your hope more entirely on Him; by His Spirit He will work in you both to will and to do.

Our single aim must be perfect harmony between conscience and conduct. Every conviction must be carried out into action. Christ's commands were meant to be obeyed. If this is not done, our accumulation of Scripture knowledge only darkens and hardens, and creates satisfaction with the pleasure which comes from acquisition of knowledge. This ruins us for the Spirit's teaching.

Do not weary of my repeating so frequently the blessed, solemn message. In your inner chamber the question must be decided whether you will, through the day, keep the commandments of Christ. And there you will decide whether or not you will bear the character of a man who lives only to know and do the will of God.

CHAPTER TWELVE

Life and Knowledge

"And out of the ground made the Lord God to grow . . . the tree of life also in the midst of the garden, and the tree of knowledge of good and evil" (Gen. 2:9).

There are two ways of knowing things. The one is in the mind by notion or conception—I know about a thing. The other is in the life—I know *by inward experience*. An intelligent blind man may know all that science teaches about light by having books read to him. Yet, a child, or a primitive, who has never thought what light is, knows it far better than the blind scholar. The former knows all about it by thinking; the latter knows it in reality by seeing and enjoying it.

It is even so in religion. The mind can form thoughts about God from the Bible, and know all the doctrines of salvation, while the inner life does not know the saving power of God. This is why we read, "He that loveth not, knoweth not God; for God is love" (1 John 4:8). He may know all about God and about love, he may be able to utter beautiful thoughts about it, but unless he loves, he does not know God. Only love can know God, and the knowledge of God is life eternal.

God's Word is the word of life. The issues of life flow out of the heart. The life may be strong, even where mental knowledge is feeble. And knowledge may be the object of pursuit and great delight, yet the life remains unaffected by it.

Suppose we could give to an apple tree understanding,

eyes and hands, thus enabling the apple tree to do for itself what the gardener now does—gather fertilizer or bring moisture. But the inner life of the apple tree would still be the same, quite different from the understanding that had been given it. So also the inner divine life in a man is extremely different from the intellect with which he knows about it. That intellect is indeed necessary for transferring to the heart the Word of God which the Holy Spirit can quicken. And yet, intellect is absolutely powerless, either to impart, or quicken, the true life. It is only a servant that carries the food; it is the *heart* that must be nourished and live.

The two trees in Eden were God's revelation of this truth. If Adam had eaten of the tree of life, he would have received and known all the good God had for him to experience. And he would have known evil only by being absolutely free from it. But Eve was led astray by the desire for knowledge—"a tree to be desired to make one wise"—and man gained a knowledge of good without possessing it; a knowledge gained from the evil that was its opposite. Since that day man has continually sought his religion more in knowledge than in life.

Only life—experience, and possession of God and His goodness—gives true knowledge. The knowledge of the intellect cannot quicken. "Though I . . . understand all mysteries, and all knowledge . . . and have not charity, I am nothing" (1 Cor. 13:2). The danger of pursuing knowledge meets us in our daily Bible reading; there it must be met and conquered. We need the intellect to hear and understand God's Word in its human meaning. But the possession of truth by the intellect cannot profit unless the Holy Spirit makes it life and truth in the heart. We need to yield our heart, and wait on God in quiet submission, trusting Him to work in us by that Spirit. As this becomes a holy habit, we shall learn the art of intellect and heart working in perfect harmony, each movement of the mind being accompanied by a corresponding movement of the heart, waiting and listening for the teaching of the Spirit.

CHAPTER THIRTEEN

The Heart and the Understanding

"Trust in the Lord with all thine heart; and lean not unto thine own understanding" (Prov. 3:5).

The chief object of the Book of Proverbs is to teach knowledge and discretion, and to guide in the path of wisdom and understanding. Proverbs offers to guide us into righteousness, the fear of the Lord, and good understanding. But it also warns us to distinguish between trusting *our own* understanding and intellect, and seeking *spiritual* understanding which God gives—an understanding heart. "Trust in the Lord with all thine heart, and lean not unto thine own understanding." As we seek after knowledge and wisdom, as we plan our life, or study the Word, we have these two powers: *the understanding or intellect,* which knows things from without (by nature and the conceptions we form), and *the heart*, which knows them by experience as it integrates them into the will and emotions.

One of the chief reasons why so much Bible teaching and Bible knowledge is comparatively fruitless, and why there is such a lack of holiness, devotion and power in the Church, is that of reliance on our own understanding for spiritual matters.

Many argue, "But surely God gave us our intellect, and without it there is no possibility of knowing God's Word." True, but listen. By the Fall, our whole human nature was disordered. The will became enslaved, the emotions were perverted, the understanding was darkened. All admit the ruin of the Fall in the two former but practically deny it in the latter. They admit that even the believer, in himself, has no power of a holy will and needs the daily renewing of the grace of Jesus Christ. They admit that he has no power of holy emotions to love God and his neighbor unless it is provided unceasingly by the Holy Spirit. But they do not recognize that the intellect is just as completely ruined and impotent, incapable of apprehending spiritual truth. It was primarily the desire for knowledge, in a method and at a time God had forbidden, that led Eve astray. Assuming that we can by ourselves take the knowledge of God's truth out of His Word as we will is still our greatest danger. We need a deep conviction of the inadequacy of our understanding to know the truth, and of the terrible danger of self-confidence and the resulting self-deception. Then we will see the need of the word, "Trust in the Lord with all thine heart; and lean not unto thine own understanding" (Prov. 3:5). With the heart man believes; with *all* the heart we are to seek, serve, and love God. Only with the heart can we know God, or worship God, in spirit and truth. It is in the heart, therefore, that the divine Word does its work. It is into our heart that God sends the Spirit of His Son. It is the heart, the inward life of desire, love, will and surrender, that the Holy Spirit guides into all the truth. In Bible study, "Trust in the Lord with all thine heart, and lean not unto thine own understanding."

Wholly distrust your own understanding. It can only give you thoughts and conceptions of divine things without the reality. It will deceive you with the thought that truth, if received into the mind, will somehow surely enter the heart. It will blind you to the terrible universal experience, that men daily read, and weekly delight to hear God's Word, and yet are made neither humble, nor holy, nor heavenly-minded.

Instead of trusting your understanding, *come with your heart* to the Bible. Instead of trusting your understanding, trust in the Lord with all your heart. Let your whole heart be set upon the living God as the Teacher when you enter your closet. Then you shall find good understanding. God will give you a heart of spiritual understanding.

You may ask, as I have been often asked, "But what am I to do? How am I to study my Bible? I see no way of doing so but by using my understanding."

Perfectly right. But do not use it for what it cannot do. Remember two things. One is, that understanding can only give you a picture or thought of spiritual things. The moment it has done this, take your heart to the Lord to make His Word life and truth in you. The other is, that pride of intellect—the danger of leaning on your own understanding—is unceasing; nothing, not even the greatest determination, can save you from this except continual dependence of the heart on the Holy Spirit's teaching. Only when the Holy Spirit quickens the Word in the heart, in the disposition and emotions, can He guide the intellect. "The meek will he guide in judgment: and the meek will he teach his way" (Ps. 25:9). "The fear of the Lord [a disposition] is the beginning of knowledge" (Prov. 1:7).

Whenever your understanding grasps a thought from the Word, bow before God in dependence and trust. Believe with your whole heart that God can and will make it true. Ask for the Holy Spirit to make it take effect in your heart. Thus the Word will become the strength of your life.

Persevere in this, and the time will come when the Holy Spirit, dwelling in your heart and life, will hold the understanding in subjection and let His holy light shine through it.

CHAPTER FOURTEEN

God's Thoughts and Our Thoughts

"As the heavens are higher than the earth, so are . . . my thoughts [higher] than your thoughts" (Isa. 55:9).

The words of a wise man often mean something different from what a hearer understands of them. How natural then that the words of God mean something infinitely higher than we initially apprehend.

Remembering this continually will prevent us from resting content with our knowledge and thoughts of the Word. Instead, we will wonder and wait for what may be its full blessing as God has meant it. It will give our prayer for the Holy Spirit's teaching new strength and urgency, as we ask Him to show us what has not yet entered into our heart to conceive. It will fortify the hope that there is, even in this life, a fulfillment beyond our highest thoughts.

God's Word thus has two meanings. One is that which is in the mind of God, making the human words the bearer of all the glory of divine wisdom, and power, and love. The other is our feeble, partial, defective apprehension of it. Even after grace and experience have made such words as "love of God," "grace of God," "power of God," or any of the many related promises, very real to us, there is still an infinite fullness in the Word we have not yet experienced.

How strikingly this is illustrated in our text from Isaiah:

"As the heavens are higher than the earth." Our faith in that fact is so simple and clear that no one would dream of trying with his arm to reach the sun or the stars. To climb the highest mountain would not help. With our whole heart we believe it. Then God says, even so, "my thoughts are higher than your thoughts." Even when the Word has shown us God's thoughts, and our thoughts have attempted to assimilate them, they still remain as high above our thoughts as the heavens are above the earth. *All the infinities of God and the eternal world dwell in the Word as the seed of eternal life.* As the full-grown oak is so mysteriously greater than the acorn from which it sprang, so God's words are but seeds from which God's mighty wonders of grace and power can grow.

Faith in this Word should teach us two lessons: the one of ignorance, the other of expectation. We should learn to come to the Word as little children. Jesus said, "Thou hast hid these things from the wise and prudent, and hast revealed them unto babes" (Matt. 11:25). The prudent and the wise are not necessarily hypocrites or enemies. Many of God's dear children, who, by neglecting to continually cultivate a childlike spirit, and unconsciously resting on the scripturalness of their creed, or the honesty of their Scripture study, have spiritual truth hidden from them, and never become spiritual men. "For what man knoweth the things of a man, save the spirit of man which is in him? Even so the things of God knoweth no man, but the Spirit of God. Now we have received . . . the spirit which is of God, that we might know" (1 Cor. 2:11, 12). Let a deep sense of our ignorance, a deep distrust of our own power of understanding the things of God, mark our Bible study.

The deeper our despair of understanding the thoughts of God, the greater our expectancy may be. God wants to make His Word true in us. "Thy children shall be taught of God." The Holy Spirit is *already* in us to reveal the things of God. In answer to our humble believing prayer God will, through Him, give ever-increasing insight into the mystery of God—our wonderful union and resemblance to Christ, His living in us, and our being as He was in this world.

In fact, if our hearts thirst and wait for it, a time may come when, by a special communication of His Spirit, all our yearnings will be satisfied; Christ will so take possession of the heart, that "as the heavens are higher than the earth, his thoughts are higher than our thoughts" will no longer be a matter of faith, but experience.

CHAPTER FIFTEEN

Meditation

"Blessed is the man . . . [whose] delight is in the law of the Lord; and in His law doth he meditate day and night" (Ps. 1:1, 2)*.

"Let the words of my mouth, and the meditation of my heart, be acceptable in thy sight, O Lord" (Ps. 19:14).

The true aim of education, study, and reading is found, not in what is brought into us, but in what is brought out of ourselves, by stimulating active exercise of our inward power. This is as true of Bible study as of any other study. God's Word only works its true blessing when the truth it brings to us stirs the inner life, and reproduces itself in resolve, trust, love, or adoration. When the heart has received the Word through the mind, and exercised its spiritual powers on it, the Word is no longer void, but has accomplished God's purpose. It has become part of our life, and strengthened us for new purpose and effort.

In meditation the heart holds and appropriates the Word. Just as in reflection the understanding grasps all the meaning and implications of a truth, so in meditation the heart assimilates it and makes it a part of its own life. The heart embodies the will and the emotions. The "meditation of the heart" implies desire, acceptance, surrender, love. Out of the heart flow the issues of life; whatever the heart truly believes, it receives with love and joy, and allows it to

---

*Also see Josh. 1:8, Ps. 119:15, 23, 48, 78, 97, 99, 148; 1 Tim. 4:15.

rule the life. The intellect gathers and prepares the "food" on which we are to feed. In meditation the heart takes it in and feeds on it.

The art of meditation needs to be cultivated. Just as a man needs to be trained to concentrate his mental powers and think clearly and accurately, a Christian needs to diligently consider and meditate until the holy habit of yielding up the whole heart to every word of God is established.

The question sometimes is asked, "How can this power of meditation be cultivated?" The very first requirement is to present ourselves before God. It is *His* Word; that Word has no power of blessing apart from Him. The Word is meant to bring us into His presence and fellowship. Practice His presence and receive the Word as from himself confident that He will make it work effectively in the heart. In Psalm 119 "meditate" is used seven times, but each time as part of a prayer addressed to God. "I will meditate in thy precepts." "Thy servant did meditate in thy statutes." "O how love I thy law! it is my meditation all the day." Meditation is the heart turning toward God, using His own Word, attempting to absorb it into the emotions and will, into its very life.

Another requirement of true meditation is quiet restfulness. As we study Scripture, endeavor to grasp an argument or to master a difficulty, our intellect often needs to expend great effort. The method required in meditation is different. Here we take a truth we have found, or some mystery for which we are awaiting divine teaching, and hide the word in the depth of the heart, believing that, by the Holy Spirit, its meaning and power will be revealed in our inner life. "Thou desirest truth in the inward parts: and in the hidden part thou shalt make me to know wisdom" (Ps. 51:6). In the description of our Lord's mother we are told: "Mary kept all these things and pondered them in her heart" (Luke 2:19). Here we have the image of a soul that has begun to know Christ, and is on the sure way to know Him better.

In meditation, personal application takes a prominent place. This is too frequently overlooked in our intellectual study of the Bible. The object of study is to know and understand. In meditation the chief object is to appropriate and experience. The true spirit of Bible study entails a readiness to believe every promise implicitly, to obey every command readily in order to "stand perfect and complete in all the will of God." It is in quiet meditation that faith is exercised, that allegiance is rendered, that full surrender to all God's will is made, and assurance received of grace to perform our vows.

Then meditation must lead to prayer. It provides subjects for prayer. It must lead on to prayer, to ask and receive definitely what it has seen or accepted in the Word. Its value is that it is the preparation for prayer which is deliberate and wholehearted supplication for what the Word has revealed as needful or possible. This requires the "rest of faith" that looks upward with assurance that the Word will open up and prove its power in the person who meekly and patiently yields himself to it.

The reward of resting for a time from intellectual effort, and cultivating the habit of holy meditation, will come in the course of time. The two will be brought into harmony, and all our study will be animated by the quiet waiting on God, and the yielding of the heart and life to the Word.

Our fellowship with God is meant to last all day. The blessing of a habit of true meditation in the morning watch will be the blessedness of the man of the first Psalm: "Blessed is the man whose delight is in the law of the Lord, and in his law doth he meditate day and night."

Workers and leaders of God's people need this more than others if they are to train them to do it and maintain their own communication with the only source of strength and blessing. God says, "I will be with thee: I will not fail thee, nor forsake thee. Only be thou strong and very courageous that thou mayest observe to do according to all the law . . . that thou mayest prosper whithersoever thou goest.

This book of the law shall not depart out of thy mouth; but thou shalt meditate therein day and night . . . and then thou shalt have good success. . . . Be strong and of a good courage" (Josh. 1:5, 7, 9).

"Let the words of my mouth, and the meditation of my heart, be acceptable *in thy sight,* O Lord, my strength and my redeemer." Let nothing less be your aim—that your meditation may be acceptable in His sight—part of the spiritual sacrifice you offer. Let nothing less be your prayer and expectation—that your meditation may be true worship—the living surrender of the heart to God's Word in His presence.

CHAPTER SIXTEEN

Revealed unto Babes

"I thank thee, O Father, Lord of heaven and earth, because thou hast hid these things from the wise and prudent, and revealed them unto babes" (Matt. 11:25; Luke 10:21).

The "wise and prudent" are people who are conscious and confident of their power of mind and reason to aid them in their pursuit of divine knowledge. The "babes" are those whose chief concern is not the mind and its power, but the heart and its disposition. Ignorance, helplessness, dependence, meekness, teachableness, trust and love—these are the attitudes God seeks in those whom He teaches (Ps. 25:9, 12, 14, 17, 20).

One of the most important elements of our devotions is the study of God's Word. When we receive the Word, we should always wait for the Father to reveal its truth in us. We should have the childlike, even the babelike disposition to which the Father loves to impart the secrets of His love. With the wise and prudent, head knowledge is the primary thing; from them God hides the spiritual meaning of the very thing they think they understand. With the babes, the heart and feeling, the sense of humility, love and trust, are primary and to them God reveals, in their inner life and experience, the very thing they know they cannot understand.

Education tells us that there are two styles of teaching. The ordinary teacher makes the communication of knowledge his chief object. He cultivates the powers of the child sufficiently to help him to attain his goal. The true teacher considers the amount of knowledge a secondary thing. His first aim is to develop the power of mind and spirit, and to aid the pupil, both mentally and morally, in using his powers properly for the pursuit and the application of knowledge. Similarly, there are two classes of preachers. Some pour out instruction and argument and application unceasingly, expecting the hearers to make the best use they can of what is presented. The true preacher understands how much depends upon the state of heart; he seeks, even as our Lord Jesus did, to subordinate the teaching of objective truth or doctrine to the cultivation of those qualities which make teaching profitable. A hundred eloquent and earnest sermons to Christians who listen, thinking that they can understand, and be profited, will bring less real blessing than one sermon to hearers in whom the preacher has awakened a consciousness of spiritual ignorance—a babelike docile spirit that waits for, depends on, and truly accepts and obeys the Father's teaching.

In the secret chamber every man must be his own teacher and preacher. He is to train himself in the blessed habit of babelike simplicity and teachableness. It is not only necessary that divine truth should be revealed in the world, but that there must be a revelation to each individual by the Holy Spirit. Therefore, his first care is to wait on the Father to reveal to him, and within him, the hidden mystery in its power in the inner life. In this posture he exercises the babelike spirit, and receives the Kingdom as a little child.

All evangelical Christians believe in regeneration. But few believe that when a man is born of God, a babelike dependence on God for all teaching and strength ought to be his chief characteristic. It was the one thing our Lord Jesus insisted on above all. He called the poor in heart, the meek and the hungry, "blessed"; He called men to learn of Him because He was meek and lowly in heart; He spoke of our humbling ourselves and becoming as little children. The first and chief mark of being a child of God, of being like Jesus Christ, is an absolute dependence upon God for every blessing, and especially for any real knowledge of spiritual things. Let each ask himself, "Have I considered the babelike spirit the first essential in my Bible study?" Of what use is Bible study without the babelike spirit? It is the only key to God's school. Set aside everything to secure this. Then God will reveal His hidden wisdom.

The new birth, by which we become God's children, is meant to make us babes. It will give us the child-spirit as well as the child-teaching. It cannot do the second without the first. Let us believe and yield ourselves to the new life in us, to the leading of the Spirit; He will breathe into us the spirit of little children. The first object of Bible study is to learn the hidden wisdom of God. The first condition of obtaining this knowledge is to accept the fact that God himself reveals it to us.

The attitude needed for receiving that revelation is a babelike spirit. We all know that the first thing a wise workman does is to see that he has the proper tools, and that they are in proper order. He does not count it lost time to stop his work and sharpen the tools. Neither is it lost time to let the Bible study wait till you see whether you are in the right position—waiting for the Father's revelation in a meek and babelike spirit. If you have not read your Bible in this spirit, confess and forsake at once the self-confident spirit of the wise and prudent. Not only pray for the babelike spirit but believe for it. It is in you, though neglected and suppressed; you may begin at once as a child of God to experience it.

Do not seek by reflection or argument to bring this babelike spirit into your heart. It must come from within. It is in you, as a seed, in the new life born of the Spirit. It must rise and grow in you as a birth of the indwelling Spirit. In this matter you must not only pray, but pray especially for this grace of the Spirit, and exercise it. Live as a babe before God. As a newborn babe desire the milk of the Word.

And beware of assuming this state of mind only when you want to study Scripture. It must be the permanent habit of your mind, the state of your heart. Then only can you enjoy the continual guidance of the Holy Spirit.

CHAPTER SEVENTEEN

Learning of Christ

"Take my yoke upon you, and learn of me; for I am
meek and lowly in heart: and ye shall find rest unto your
souls" (Matt. 11:29).

All Bible study is learning. All Bible study, to be fruitful, should be learning of Christ. The Bible is the school-
book, Christ is the teacher. It is He who opens the understanding, and opens the heart, and opens the seals (Luke
24:45; Acts 16:14; Rev. 5:9). Christ is the living eternal
Word, of which the written words are the human expression. Christ's presence and teaching are the secret of all
true Bible study. The written Word is powerless, except as
it leads us to the living Word. No one has ever thought of
accusing our Lord of not honoring the Old Testament. In
His own life He proved that He loved it as coming out of the
mouth of God. He always pointed the Jews to it as the revelation of God and the witness to himself. But with the disciples He frequently spoke of His own teaching as what they
most needed, and had to obey. Only after His resurrection,
when the union with Christ had been effected, and they had
already received the first breathings of the Spirit (John
20:22), do we find Him expounding the Scriptures. The
Jews had their self-made interpretation of the Word; they
made it the greatest barrier between themselves and Him of
whom it spoke. This is common with Christians, too; our
human apprehension of Scripture, fortified as it may be by
the authority of the Church, or our own circle, becomes the

greatest hindrance to Christ's teachings. Christ the living Word, seeks first to find His place in our heart and life, to be our only teacher; then we can learn from Him to honor and understand Scripture.

"Learn of me, for I am meek and lowly of heart." Here our Lord reveals the inmost secret of His own inner life. That which He brought down to us from heaven; that which fits Him to be a teacher and a Savior; that which He has given to us, and which He wants us to learn, is all found in the words, "I am meek and lowly of heart." This one virtue makes Him the Lamb of God, our suffering Redeemer, our heavenly teacher and leader. It is the one attitude which He asks of us in coming to learn from Him; from this, all else will come. For Bible study and all Christian life, here is the one condition of truly learning of Christ. He, the teacher, meek and lowly of heart, wants to *make you what He is,* because *that is salvation.* As a learner you must come and study and believe in Him, the meek and lowly One, and seek to learn from Him how to be meek and lowly too.

And why is this the first and all-important issue? Because it lies at the root of the true relationship of the creature to God. God alone has life and goodness and happiness. As the God of love He delights to give and work everything in us. Christ became the Son of Man to show what blessed unceasing dependence upon God man is to have; this is the meaning of being "lowly in heart." In this spirit the angels veil their faces and cast their crowns before God. God is everything to them, and they delight to receive all and to give all. This is the root of the true Christian life—to be nothing before God and men; to wait on God alone; to delight in, to imitate, to learn of Christ, the meek and lowly one. This is the key to the School of Christ, the only key to the true knowledge of Scripture. With this attitude Christ has come to teach: it is only with this attitude you can learn of Him. In the Christian Church, humility—the meek and lowly heart—has not had the importance that it has in the life of Christ and the teachings of God's Word. I am certain that this lack has caused a very large part of the feebleness and unfruitfulness of which we hear. Only as we are meek and lowly in heart can Christ teach us by His Spirit what God has for us, and can God work in us. Let each of us begin with ourselves and count this as the first condition of discipleship, and the first lesson the Master will most surely teach us. Let us make all our Bible study a learning of Christ. We must trust Him, who is so meek, gentle and kind, and wait for Him to work His own spirit and likeness in us. In due time our morning watch will be the scene of daily fellowship and daily blessing.

The meek and lowly heart must be made the first consideration in Bible study. In communion with God, attitude and character are everything. Of all Christian attitudes and character, a meek and lowly heart is the very seed and root; without it the profit of Bible study is very little. The meek and lowly heart can be possessed because it is the very thing Christ offers to give, teaching us how to find and receive it in himself. I urge all Bible students, thoughtfully and prayerfully to first settle this question in the inner chamber: "Is my heart in the condition in which my Teacher desires it to be? If not, is not my first responsibility to yield myself to Him to develop it in me?"

CHAPTER EIGHTEEN

Teachableness

"Take my yoke upon you and learn of me; for I am meek and lowly in heart; and ye shall find rest unto your souls" (Matt. 11:29).

The first quality of a pupil is docility and willingness to be taught. This implies consciousness of his own ignorance, a readiness to give up his own way of thinking or doing and to examine things from the teacher's standpoint, a quiet confidence that the master "knows" and will show him how to learn to "know" also. The meek and lowly spirit listens carefully to understand what the teacher's will is, and immediately hastens to carry it out. If this is the spirit in a pupil, it will be the teacher's fault if he does not learn.

But how is it that, with Christ as our teacher, there is with many so much failure, so little real growth in spiritual knowledge? So much hearing and reading of the Bible and profession of faith in it as our only rule of life, and yet so little manifestation of its spirit and its power? So much earnest application in the closet and the study group, with so little of the joy and strength God's Word could give?

There must be some reason why so many disciples of Jesus, who think they honestly desire to know and do His will, by their own confession and the evidence of those around them, are not displaying the word of life as a light in the world. If the answer could be found to the question, their lives might be changed.

Our text presents the answer: "Take my yoke upon you

and learn of me; for I am meek and lowly of heart: and ye shall find rest unto your souls." Many have taken Christ as a Savior but not as a teacher. They have put their trust in Him as the Good Shepherd who gave His life for the sheep, but they know little of the reality of His daily shepherding His flock, calling every one by name, or of hearing His voice and following Him. They know little of what it is to follow the Lamb—to receive from Him the lamb nature, and to seek to be meek and lowly in heart like Him. It was by their three-year course in His school that Christ's disciples were fitted for the baptism of the Holy Spirit, and the fulfillment of all the wonderful promises He had given them. Under the personal teaching of our Lord Jesus, and through the docility of the meek and lowly heart, which daily waits for, receives and follows that teaching, we can truly find rest for our souls. All the weariness and burden of strain and failure and disappointment will give way to that divine peace which knows that all is being cared for by Christ himself.

We must take Christ's yoke and learn of Him—His meekness and lowliness of heart, and the teachableness that refuses to know or do anything in its own wisdom. This should be the spirit of our whole life, every day and all the day. It is especially in the morning hour that this is to be cultivated, and deliverance is to be sought from self and all its energy. It is there, while occupied with the words of God, of Christ, and of the Holy Spirit that we need to realize that these only profit as they lead to, and are opened up by, the personal teaching of Christ. It is there that we daily need to experience that as the living Lord Jesus—"in whom all the fulness dwells," in whom all our life and salvation depend—comes near and takes charge of us, His teaching can then be received. And it is there that we must ask for and cultivate the teachableness that takes up His yoke and learns of Him. *Teachableness is everything.* If it be true that the Holy Spirit who dwells in us "shall teach you all things," and if His whole purpose in us is that of divine teaching, it is equally true that our whole purpose must be that of divine teachableness. Then only can our daily communion with God's Word, and our daily life, be what our Lord Jesus desires to make it.

"Unlearning" is often the most important part of learning; wrong impressions, prejudices and presuppositions are insurmountable obstacles to learning. Until these have been removed the teacher labors in vain. The knowledge he communicates only touches the surface; deep under the surface the pupil is guided by that which has become second nature to him. The first work of the teacher is to expose, then make the pupil see and remove those hindrances.

We can gain no true and fruitful learning of Christ if we are not ready to unlearn. By heredity, education and tradition, we have ideas about religion and God's Word, which are often the greatest hindrance because of our assurance that they are indeed the truth. Learning of Christ requires a willingness to subject every truth we hold to His inspection for criticism and correction.

Humility is the root virtue of the Christian life. The law is absolute in God's Kingdom: "He that humbleth himself shall be exalted" (Luke 14:11). Our disappointment in striving after higher degrees of grace, faith, spiritual knowledge, love for others and power to bless is all owing to this. We have not accepted the humility of Christ as the beginning and the perfection of His salvation. "God giveth grace to the humble" has a far wider and deeper application than we think.

Docility is one form of humility. In the morning watch we place ourselves as learners in Christ's school; let docility—humility—be the distinguishing mark of the learner. If we sense this is lacking, let us listen to the voice that says, "Take my yoke upon you," and, for all that this implies, "learn of me; for I am meek and lowly in heart: and ye shall find rest unto your souls."

CHAPTER NINETEEN

The Life and the Light

"In the beginning was the Word . . . and the Word was God. In him was life; and the life was the light of men" (John 1:1, 4).

"He that followeth me shall not walk in darkness, but shall have the light of life" (John 8:12).

Because Christ was God, He could be the Word of God. Because He had the life of God in himself, He could be the revealer of that Life. And so as the living Word He is the life-giving Word. The written Word can be made void and ineffective when human wisdom is trusted for its understanding. Only as it is accepted as the seed in which the life of the living Word is hidden, to be quickened by the Holy Spirit can it be to us the word of life. Our interaction with God's written Word ought to be inspired and regulated by the faith of the Eternal Word, "who was God."

The same truth is embodied in the expression, "the life is the light." When we see light shining, we know that there is fire burning in some form or other. And so in the spiritual world. There must be life before there can be light. A dead or dark object may borrow light and reflect it, but true life alone can show true light. He that follows Christ "shall have the light of life."

These two statements of one great truth strikingly confirm what we have learned about the Spirit of God. Even as He knows the things of God because He is the life of God, so Christ is the Word because He is God, and has the life of

God; so also the light of God only shines where the life of God is. All three thoughts bring us again to our Bible study with the one needful lesson; it is only as the written Word brings us the life of the Eternal Word, and as the Holy Spirit who knows the things of God makes them life and truth within us, that our study of Scripture can really bless us.

And so we return to the one great lesson the Spirit seeks to enforce in regard to God's Word: only as Scripture is received out of the life of God into our life can there be any real knowledge of it. It is a seed that bears within it the divine life; when it is received in the good soil of a heart that hungers for that life, it will spring up and bring forth fruit, like all seed, "after its kind." It will reproduce in our life the very life of God, the very likeness and disposition of the Father, and the Son, through the Holy Spirit. We want to make this very practical and apply it directly to our private Bible reading. You want to know how to begin. The rules are very simple.

First, "Be still and know that I am God." Take time to be quiet and to comprehend God. "Hold thy peace at the presence of the Lord." "Be silent before the Lord." "The Lord is in his holy temple; let all the earth keep silence before him." Worship and wait on Him that He may speak to you.

Next, remember that the word comes out of the life; the heart of God carries His life to impart it to yours. This is nothing less than the life of God; nothing less than the power of God can make it live in you.

Next, believe in Christ the living Word. "In him was life; and the life [His life] was the light of men." "He that followeth *me* shall . . . have the light of life." Follow Jesus in love and longing desire, in obedience and service; His life will work in you, and the life shall be the light of your soul.

Finally, ask the Father for the Holy Spirit, who alone knows the things of God, to make the Word in your heart living and active. Hunger for the will of God as your daily food. Thirst for the living spring of the Spirit within you. Receive the Word into your will, your life, your joy. The life it brings will give the light with which it shines.

The reason I have so frequently repeated this truth in the last few chapters is very simple. My own experience has taught me how long it takes before we understand that the Word of God must be received into the life—not only into the mind—and how long it takes for us to fully believe and act it out. "To write the same things to you to me indeed is not grievous, but for you it is safe" (Phil. 3:1). Study the lesson till you know it. The word comes out of the life of God, carries that life in itself, and seeks to enter my life and fill it with the life of God. This life is the light of men, and gives the light of the knowledge of the glory of God.

You may find that this lesson takes more time than you think, that it hinders more than it helps in your Bible lessons, and that it becomes more difficult the longer you study it. Do not be afraid or impatient; be assured that if you learn it properly, you will bless God for this key to the hidden treasure of the Word, which gives you true wisdom in the hidden part.

As only the Spirit that lives in God knows the things of God, it is only the Spirit living in me that can make me know the things of God by imparting them to my life.

As Christ was the Word because He was God, and had the life of God, the written Word can only bless me as, through it, the living Word brings the life of God to me. As the life was in Christ, and as the life is the light of men, so it is only as I have the life of Christ through the Word that I have the light of the knowledge of God.

CHAPTER TWENTY

The Bible Student

"Blessed is the man . . . [whose] delight is in the law of
the Lord; and in his law doth he meditate day and night"
(Ps. 1:1, 2).

There is a loud call on every side for more and genuine
Bible study. Evangelists like Mr. Moody and many others
have proved what power there is in preaching based solely
on God's Word and inspired by faith in its power. Con-
cerned Christians have resultantly asked, "Why can't our
ministers speak in the same way, giving the Word of God
greater emphasis?" Many a young minister has come away
from the seminary, confessing that he had been taught everything but the knowledge of how to study the Word and
stir up and help others to study it. In some of our churches
the desire has been voiced to meet this need in the training
of ministers. It would appear very simple to find good men
to undertake the work; yet, it has been found difficult for
men with theological training to change and simply consult
God's Word. This is necessary if they are to show younger
men the way to make Scripture the one source of their
knowledge and teaching. In the students' movement of our
day, Bible study has been given the place of prominence.
There is a wonderful opportunity, as there is a very great
need, for giving God's Word its true place in the work to be
done for Him. Let us consider the principles underlying the
demand for more Bible study.

1. *God's Word is the only authentic revelation of God's
will.* All human statements of divine truth, however cor-

rect, are defective and carry a measure of human authority. In the Word, the voice of God speaks to us directly. Every child of God is called to direct communion with the Father through the Word. As God reveals all His heart and grace in it, His child can, if he receives it from God, get all the life and power in the Word into his own heart and being. Few secondhand reports of messages or events can be fully trusted. Very few men report accurately what they have heard. Every believer, therefore, has the right and calling to live in direct communication with God. In the Word God has revealed, and in the Word He still reveals, himself to each individual.

2. *This Word of God is a living Word. It carries a divine quickening power in it.* The human expression of the truth is often a mere conception or image of the truth, appealing to the mind and having little or no effect. Faith that the word is God's own word, with His presence and power in it, makes it effective. All life or spirit creates for itself a form in which it is made manifest. The words in which God has chosen to clothe His own divine thoughts are God-breathed and the life of God dwells in them. God is not the God of the dead but of the living. The Word was not only inspired when first given; the Spirit of God still breathes in it. God is still in and with His Word. Christians and teachers need to believe this. It will lead them to give the simple divine Word a credence that no human teaching may have.

3. *God alone can, and most surely will, be the interpreter of His own Word.* Divine truth needs a divine teacher. Spiritual apprehension of spiritual things can come only from the Holy Spirit. The more one is convinced of the unique character of the Word (essentially different from, and infinitely exalted above all merely human apprehension), the more urgently he will feel the need of a supernatural, directly divine teaching. And all the more will he realize the blessing, because that is the great purpose of the Word. The soul will be brought to seek God himself, and it will find Him in the Holy Spirit who dwells in the heart. As that Spirit, by whom God has entered our life, is waited on

and trusted, He will teach us wisdom in the hidden part, in the heart and disposition. The Word prayerfully read and cherished in the heart with such faith will, through the Spirit, be both light and life within us.

4. *The Word then brings us into the closest and most intimate fellowship with God—unity of will and life.* In the Word God has revealed His whole heart and all His will. In His law and precepts He reveals what He wills us to do; in His redemption and His promises He reveals what He wills to do for us. As we accept that will in the Word as from God himself, and yield ourselves to its effect, we learn to know God in His will. We learn to know Him in the power with which He works in us, the power in which His condescending love is known. And the Word fulfills His richest purpose when it fills us with the reverence and dependence that come from the divine presence. We must aim for and experience nothing less in all our Bible study.

Let us now review these four thoughts and make practical application.

1. In Holy Scripture we have the very words in which the Holy God has spoken, and in which He speaks to us.

2. These words are, today, full of the life of God. God is in them, and makes His presence and power known to them who seek Him in the Word.

3. To those who ask and wait for the teaching of the Holy Spirit who dwells within us, the Spirit will reveal the spiritual meaning and power of the Word.

4. The Word is thus meant to be the daily means of the revelation of God himself and of fellowship with Him.

Have we learned to apply these truths? Do we understand that the Word says, "Seek God. Hearken to God. Wait for God. God will speak to you. Let God teach you"? All we hear about more Bible teaching and Bible study must lead to this one thing. We must be people, and we must train others to be people who never separate the Word from the living God himself. We must live as people to whom God in heaven speaks every day and all day.

CHAPTER TWENTY-ONE

Who Art Thou?

"Set your affection on things above, . . . for ye are
dead, and your life is hid with Christ in God" (Col. 3:2, 3).

When entering into God's presence in the morning hour,
much depends upon the Christian realizing not only who
God is but who he is, and what his relation to God is. The
question, "Who art thou?" is asked, not in words but in
spirit, of each one who claims right of access and an audi-
ence from the Most High. He must have an answer ready in
his inmost consciousness; that consciousness must be a living sense of the place he has in Christ before God. The
mode of expressing it may differ at various times, but in
substance it will always be the same.

Who am I? Let me think and say who I am as I come to
ask that God shall meet me here and spend this whole day
with me. I am one who knows, by the Word and Spirit of
God, that I am in Christ and that my life is hid with Christ
in God. In Christ I died to sin and the world. I am now tak-
en out of them, separated from them and delivered from
their power. I have been raised together with Christ and in
Him I live unto God. My life is hid with Christ in God and I
come to God to claim and obtain all divine life that is hidden away in Him for today's needs.

"Yes, this is who I am," I say to God in humble, holy
reverence, as my plea. Seek and expect nothing less than
grace to live out, here on earth, the hidden life of heaven. I
am one who says, "Christ is my life." The longing of my

soul is for Christ to be revealed by the Father himself within my heart. Nothing less can satisfy me. My life is hid with Christ. He can be my life no other way than as He is in my heart. I can be content with nothing less than Christ in my heart—Christ as a Savior from sin, Christ as the gift and bringer of God's love, Christ as an indwelling Friend and Lord.

Oh, my God, if you ask, "Who art thou?" listen to my stammering. I live in Christ and Christ lives in me. You alone can make me know and be all it means.

My plea is for the grace of God's presence and power all the day. I come desiring, seeking preparation to live out the life of Christ today on earth, to translate His hidden heavenly glory into the language of daily life. As the Christ on earth lived only to do the will of God, I desire to stand perfect and complete in all His will. My ignorance of that will, and all its spiritual application to association with the world and men, is very great. My impotence is still greater. And yet I come to God as one who dares not offer less or seek any compromise. In all honesty I accept the high calling of living out fully the will of God in all things.

This brings me to the closet. I think of all my failures in fulfilling God's will; I look ahead to all the temptations and dangers that await me; I feel my entire insufficiency and yet say to God, "I come to claim the life hid in Christ that I may live my life for Christ; I will not be content without the quiet assurance that God will go with me and bless me."

Who am I that I should ask these great and wonderful things of God? May I expect to live the life hid with Christ in God and manifest it in my mortal body? I may, for God himself will work it in me through the Holy Spirit dwelling in me. The same God who raised Christ from the dead, and then set Him at His right hand, has raised me with Him. He has given me the Spirit of the glory of His Son in my heart. A life in Christ, given up to know and do all God's will, is the life God himself will increasingly develop and maintain in me by the Holy Spirit. I come in the morning and present myself before Him to take up afresh the life He has hidden in himself for me, and to live it out in the flesh. I can wait confidently and quietly, as one in whom the Spirit dwells, for the Father to give the fresh anointing that teaches all things, and to take charge of the new day He has given me.

I am sure you feel how important it is, if the morning hour is to secure God's presence for the day, that you take a firm stand on the ground of a full redemption. Believe what God says to you. Accept what God has bestowed on you in Christ. Be consciously and openly what God has made you to be. Take time before God to know it and say it. Victory in a battle depends upon an impregnable position. Take your place in Christ.

The very attempt to do this may at times interfere with your ordinary Bible study or prayer. It will be no loss. You will be fully compensated later. Your whole life depends upon knowing who your God is, and who you are as His redeemed one in Christ. The life of every day depends on it. Once you have learned the secret, it will, even when you do not think of it, be the strength of your heart, both in going in to God and going out with Him to the world.

CHAPTER TWENTY-TWO

The Will of God

"Thy will be done in earth, as it is in heaven" (Matt. 6:10).

1. The will of God is the living power to which the world owes its existence. Through that will, and according to that will, the world is what it is. It is the expression or embodiment of that Divine Will in its wisdom, power and goodness. What it has in beauty and glory, it owes to God's having willed it. As that Will formed it, so it upholds it every day. Creation thus does what it was destined for: it shows forth the glory of God. "[They gave] glory . . . to him . . . who liveth for ever and ever . . . saying, Thou art worthy . . . to receive glory . . . for thou hast created all things, and for thy pleasure they are and were created" (Rev. 4:9-11).

2. This is true of inanimate nature. It is even more true of intelligent creatures. The Divine Will created a creature-will in its own image and likeness, with the living power to know, accept, and co-operate with that Will to which it owes its being. The unfallen angels count it their highest honor and happiness to be able to will and do exactly what God wills and does. The glory of heaven is that God's will is done there. The sin and misery of fallen angels and men consists simply in their having turned away from, and having refused to abide in, and do, the will of God.

3. Redemption is simply the restoration of God's will to its place in the world. To this end Christ came and showed

in a human life that man has but one thing to live for, the doing of God's will. He showed us how there was one way of conquering self-will—by a death to it, in obeying God's will even unto death. So He atoned for our self-will and conquered it for us, thus opening a path through death and resurrection into a life entirely united with, and devoted to, the will of God.

4. God's redeeming will is now able to do in fallen man what His creating will had wrought and ever works in nature and in unfallen beings. Through Christ and His example, God has revealed the devotion to and the delight in His will, which He expects of us. In Christ and His Spirit He renews and takes possession of our will; He works in it both to will and to do, making us able and willing to do all His desire.

He himself does all things after the counsel of His will. He makes "you perfect in every good work to do his will, working in you that which is well-pleasing in his sight" (Heb. 13:21). As this is revealed by the Holy Spirit and received into the heart, we begin to gain insight into the prayer, "Thy will be done in earth, as it is in heaven," and desire is awakened for the life it promises.

5. It is essential to the believer that he realize his relationship to God's will and its claim on him. Many believers have no conception of what their faith or their feeling ought to be in regard to the will of God. How few say, "My whole concept of blessedness is that of complete harmony with the will of God." My one need is to be so surrendered as to never do other than what God wills me to do. By God's grace every hour of my life may be spent living in the will of God, doing it as it is done in heaven.

6. Only as the Divine Will, increasingly working out its purposes in us, masters the heart, shall we have the courage to believe in the answer to the prayer our Lord taught us. Only when we see that it is through Jesus Christ that God's will is carried out in us shall we understand how the close

union with Him gives the confidence that God will work all in us. Only this confidence in God, through Jesus Christ, will assure us that we, too, can do our part, and that our feeble will on earth can ever correspond and co-operate with the will of God. Let us allow our destiny, and our obligation to become the one thing our heart desires, that in everything the will of God may be done in us and by us as it is done in heaven. Then faith will overcome the world.

7. The will may not be disconnected from its living union with the Father, nor the living presence of the Blessed Son. Only by a divine guidance given through the Holy Spirit can the will of God in its beauty, in its application to daily life, in its ever-growing revelation, be truly known. This instruction will be given, not to the wise and prudent, but to the babes, the men of childlike disposition, who are willing to wait for and depend on what is given them. The divine guidance will lead in the path of God's will.

8. Our secret communion with God is the place where we repeat and learn the great lesson:

(a) The God whom I worship expects of me perfect union with His will.

(b) My worship means, "I delight to do thy will, O God."

(c) As I seek and cultivate the knowledge of God's will and the power to perform it, during my secret communion with God, my study of God's Word and my prayer will bring their true and full blessing.

CHAPTER TWENTY-THREE

Feeding on the Word

"Thy words were found, and I did eat them; and thy word was unto me the joy and rejoicing of mine heart" (Jer. 15:16).

Here we see three stages. The first is the *finding* of God's word. This only comes to those who seek diligently for it. Then comes the *eating*. This is personal appropriation for our own sustenance, the taking up into our being the words of God. "Man shall not live by bread alone, but by every word that proceedeth out of the mouth of God" (Matt. 4:4). Finally comes the *rejoicing*. "The kingdom of heaven is like unto treasure hid in a field; the which when a man hath found, he hideth, and for joy thereof goeth and selleth all that he hath, and buyeth that field" (Matt. 13:44). In this passage also, we have the finding, the appropriating, and the rejoicing. "Thy words were found, and I did eat them; and thy word was unto me the joy and rejoicing of my heart."

Eating is the central thought. It is preceded by the searching and finding; and is accompanied and followed by the rejoicing. Eating is the only aim of searching; it is the only cause and life of rejoicing. In the secrecy of the inner chamber much depends on "I did eat them."

To understand the difference between eating and finding God's words, compare the grain a man has stored in his granary with the bread he has on his table. All the diligent labor he has expended in sowing, harvesting, and storing his grain, all the satisfaction he has gained from his work, cannot profit him unless he feeds on the daily portion of the bread his body requires. The finding—the harvesting and storing the high yield and efficient work—are only the things to be looked at. In the eating, the very opposite takes place; here the small quantity, and slow and unceasing perseverance, characterizes the appropriation. Do you see the application of this to your Scripture study in the morning watch? You need to find God's words, and by careful thought master them so as to have them stored in mind and memory for your own use and that of others. In this work there may often be great joy, the joy of harvest or of victory; the joy of treasure secured, or difficulties overcome. Yet, we must remember that finding and possessing the words of God is not *eating* them, which alone brings divine life and strength to the soul.

Being occupied with, and possessing good wholesome grain, will not nourish a man. Neither will being deeply interested in the knowledge of God's Word nourish the soul. "Thy words were found" was the first thing, but "I did eat them" brought the joy and rejoicing.

What is this eating? The grain which the farmer had grown and rejoiced in as his very own could not nourish his life until he took it up, ate it, and completely assimilated it so that it became part of himself, entering his blood and forming his very bone and flesh. This must be done in small quantities, two or three times a day, every day of the year. This is the law of eating. It is not the amount of truth I gather from God's Word; it is not the interest or success of my Bible study; it is not the increased clarity or largeness of grasp I am obtaining that insure the health and growth of my spiritual life. All these often leave the person very much unsanctified and unspiritual, with very little of the holiness or humility of Christ Jesus. Something else is needed.

Jesus said, "My meat is to do the will of him that sent me." Take a small portion of God's Word—some definite command or duty of the new life—quietly receiving it into the will and the love of the heart, yielding the whole being to its rule, and vowing, in the power of the Lord Jesus, to perform it; then obey it. This is eating the Word, taking it into our inmost being, so that it becomes an integral part of our very life. Do the same with a truth, or a promise; what you have eaten becomes part of yourself, and is carried with you where you go as part of the life you live.

You see how the two points of difference between the grain in the granary and the bread on the table cover all your Bible study. Gathering Scripture knowledge is one thing. Eating God's Word, receiving it into your very heart by the power of the life-giving Spirit, is something very different. And you see how the two laws of eating the food, in contrast to those of finding it, must always be obeyed. You can gather and garner grain to last for years, but you cannot swallow a large enough quantity of bread to last for days. Day by day, and more than once a day, you take your day's food. So also the eating of God's Word must be in small portions, only as much as the soul can each time receive and digest. And this, day by day, from one end of the year to the other.

Such feeding on the Word will enable you to say, "And thy word was unto me the joy and rejoicing of mine heart." George Muller said he learned that he should never stop reading the Word until he felt happy in God; then he felt fit to face his day's work.

CHAPTER TWENTY-FOUR

Vacations

"If the goodman of the house had known what hour the thief would come, he would have watched, and not have suffered his house to be broken through" (Luke 12:39).

The renowned British educator, Edward Thring, said, "The mighty leisure hours with their occupations are all-powerful. . . . The mighty question of leisure hours ought to be the most important question of all, since it affects our character most. . . . Leisure hours are the hinge on which true education turns." This eminent authority in the field of education had seen that noble character and authentic being come first; after that, as second, the training of skill and strength. He had seen, too, that though a teacher can do much by high belief and true work to stimulate and to guide, every student has to develop his own character. It is in the leisure hours, when free from constraint and observation, that the student shows what is really uppermost within him. Therefore Thring spoke of the leisure hours as all-important and all-powerful, "the hinge on which true education turns."

In spiritual life this is intensely true. Thousands of students have felt it, without knowing how to express or explain it. At college or school their morning watch has been regularly observed. The whole mind is inclined toward regular and systematic work; thus the time for devotion is as duly kept as that for a class or private study.

When the time of relaxation comes, and one is free to do

exactly as one likes, many a student finds that the morning watch and its fellowship with God had not become so natural, so necessary for spiritual life and joy. Therefore, observance is not included with vacation pleasure. The vacation becomes the test of character, the proof of whether one could say with Job, "I have esteemed the words of his mouth more than my necessary food." The question of leisure hours is crucial. In them one turns freely and naturally to what he loves most. In them one proves and increases the power to keep what he has.

A teacher in a large school in America reportedly said, "The greatest difficulty with which we have to contend is the summer vacation. Just when we have brought a student up to a good point of discipline, and he responds to the best ideals, we lose him; when he comes back in the autumn, we have to begin and do it all over. The summer holiday simply demoralizes him." This statement, referring to secular study and duty, is strong; within certain limits it is just as applicable to the spiritual life. The sudden relaxation of regular habits, and the subtle thought that perfect liberty to do as one likes means perfect happiness, throws many a young student backward in his Christian life. There is no point at which it is more necessary for older and more experienced members of students' fellowships to help and guard their younger members. The progress of months may be lost by the neglect of a week. We know not in what hour the thief will come. The spirit of the morning watch means unceasing vigilance *all* the day and *every* day.

There are various aspects which may be emphasized in order to warn the student. During vacation we are set free from the school laws under which we live during our stay there. But there are *other* laws: laws of morality, laws of health, from which there is no relaxation. Warn the student that the call to daily fellowship with God belongs not to the former but the latter category. As much as he needs during the vacation to daily eat and breathe, he needs to daily eat the bread and breathe the air of heaven.

Emphasize that the morning watch is not only a duty, but an unspeakable privilege and pleasure. Fellowship with God, abiding in Christ, loving the Word and meditating on it all the day are life and strength, health and gladness to the new nature. They should look upon them in this light, believe in the power of the new nature within, and act upon it. If they count it a joy, it will become a joy to them.

Above all, they must realize that the world needs them and depends on them to be its light. Christ is waiting for them as members of His body, day by day, to do His saving work through them. Neither he, nor the world, nor they can afford to lose a single day.

God has created and redeemed you that through you He may, as through the sun He illuminates the world, shine His light and life and love upon men. You need to be in communication with the fountain of all light daily. Do not think of asking for a vacation relief from this communion, much less take it. Prize your vacation for the special opportunity of more fellowship with the Father and the Son. Don't allow it to become a snare, and exhaust all your energy in just keeping from losing ground. Prize the vacation as a blessed time for grace and victory over self and the world, of great increase of grace and strength, of being blessed and being made a blessing.

CHAPTER TWENTY-FIVE

The Inward and the Outward

"Ye fools, did not he that made that which is without, make that which is within also?" (Luke 11:40).

Every spirit seeks to create for itself a form or shape in which to embody its life, the outward being the visible expression of the hidden inward life. The outward is generally known before the inward; through it the inward is developed and reaches its full perfection, as the apostle says in 1 Cor. 15:46, "Howbeit that was not first which is spiritual, but that which is natural, and afterward that which is spiritual." To understand and maintain the right relation between the inward and the outward is one of the greatest secrets of the Christian life.

If Adam in paradise had not listened to the tempter, his trial would have resulted in the perfection of his inward life. His sin, his ruin, and all his misery came because he gave himself up to the power of the visible outward world. Instead of seeking his happiness in the hidden inward life of obedience, love, and dependence, he fixed his desire on the world around him, on the pleasure and the knowledge of good and evil that it could give him.

All false religion, from the most degrading idolatry to the corruption of Judaism and Christianity, has its root in what is outward. What can please the eye, interest the mind, or gratify the taste displaces that truth in the inward part, that hidden wisdom in the heart and life, which God seeks and gives.

The great characteristic of the New Testament is that it is a dispensation of the inner life. The promise of the new covenant is, "I will put my law in their inward parts, and write it in their hearts" (Jer. 31:33); "A new heart also will I give you, and a new spirit will I put within you. . . . And I will put my spirit within you" (Ezek. 36:26). The promise of our Lord Jesus was, "The Spirit of truth . . . shall be in you. At that day ye shall know that I am . . . in you" (John 14:17, 20). It is in a heart into which God has deposited the Spirit of His Son, a heart in which the love of God is shed abroad, that true salvation is found. The inner chamber, with its secret communion with the Father, "who seeth in secret," is the symbol and the training school of the inner life. Sincere and faithful daily use of the inner chamber will make the inner hidden life strong and glad.

In all our religion the great danger is giving more time and interest to the outward means than the inward reality. It is neither the intensity of your Bible study, nor the frequency or fervency of your prayers or good works that necessarily constitute a true spiritual life. We need to realize that as God is a Spirit so there is a spirit within us that can know and receive Him, become conformed to His likeness, and partake of the very dispositions that animate Him as God in His goodness and love.

Firmly settle this in your mind, that all our salvation consists in the manifestation of the nature, life, and spirit of Christ Jesus in our outward and inward new man. This alone renews and regains the first life of God in the soul of man. Wherever you go, whatever you do, at home or abroad, do all with a desire for union with Christ, in imitation of His character and inclinations. Desire nothing so much as that which exercises and increases the spirit and life of Christ in your soul, and to have everything within you changed into the character and spirit of the holy Jesus.

Consider the treasure you have within you—the Savior of the world, the eternal Word of God, hidden in your heart as a seed of the divine nature—which is to overcome sin and death within you and generate the life of heaven in your soul. Turn to your heart, and your heart will find its Savior, its God, within itself. You see and feel nothing of God because you seek for Him elsewhere, in books, in the church, in outward activities; but there you will not find Him till you have first found Him in your heart. Seek for Him in your heart and you will never seek in vain, for there He dwells, there are His light and Holy Spirit.

CHAPTER TWENTY-SIX

The Daily Renewal—Its Power

"Though our outward man perish, yet the inward man is renewed day by day" (2 Cor. 4:16).

"According to his mercy he saved us, by the washing of regeneration, and renewing of the Holy Ghost" (Titus 3:5).

With every new day the life of nature is renewed. As the sun rises again with its light and warmth, the flowers open, and the birds sing, and life is everywhere stirred and strengthened. As we rise from sleep and eat our morning food, we feel that we have gathered new strength for the duties of the day. The inner chamber is the established confession that our inward life needs daily renewal too. Only by fresh nourishment from God's Word, and fresh communion with God himself in prayer, can the vigor of the spiritual life be maintained and grow. Though our outward man perish, though the burden of sickness or suffering, the strain of work and weariness may exhaust or weaken us, the inward man can be renewed daily.

A quiet time and place, with the Word and prayer, are the means of the renewal. But these are effective only when the divine power works through them. That power is the Holy Spirit, the mighty power of God "that worketh in us." Our study of the inner chamber, and the inner life it represents, would be defective if we did not emphasize the daily renewal of the inward man, which the blessed Spirit performs. The text from Titus teaches that we have been saved "by the washing of regeneration, and renewing of the Holy

Ghost." The two expressions are not meant to be redundant. The regeneration is one great act, the beginning of the Christian life; the renewing of the Holy Ghost is a work that is carried on continuously. In Romans 12:2 we read of the progressive transformation of the Christian life that comes by "the renewing of the mind." In Ephesians 4:22, 23, the word "put off . . . the old man" (in the aorist) indicates an act done once for all, but the word "be renewed in the spirit of your mind" is in the present tense and indicates a progressive work. Even so in Colossians 3:10 we read, you "have put on the new man, which *is* [not, 'has been'] renewed . . . in the image of him that created him." We are to look to the blessed Spirit on whom we can count for the daily renewal of the inner man in the inner chamber.

Everything depends, in our private devotions, upon our maintaining the true relation to the third person of the blessed Trinity; through Him alone, the Father and the Son can do their work of saving love; through Him alone the Christian can do his work. That relation may be expressed in the two simple words, *faith* and *surrender*.

Faith. Scripture says, "God hath sent forth the Spirit of his Son into your hearts, crying, Abba, Father" (Gal. 4:6). The very feeblest child of God who desires in his morning devotion to offer up prayer that shall please the Father, and bless himself, must remember that he has received the Holy Spirit as the spirit of prayer; His help is indispensable to enable us to pray effectually. Even so with the Word of God. By the Holy Spirit alone can the truth in its divine meaning and power be revealed to us and do its work in our heart. If the daily renewal of the inward man in the morning hour is to be a reality, take time to meditate, and to worship, and to believe with your whole heart that the Holy Spirit has been given you; He is within you, and through Him God will work the blessing which He gives through prayer and the Word.

Surrender. Do not forget that the Holy Spirit must have

entire control. "As many as are led by the Spirit of God, they are the sons of God" (Rom. 8:14). They walk after the Spirit, not after the flesh. It is the ungrieved presence of the Spirit that gives the Word its light and power and keeps us in that blessed life of childlike confidence and childlike obedience which pleases God. Praise God for this wonderful gift, the Holy Spirit in His renewing power, and look with new joy and hope to the inner chamber as the place where the inner man can indeed be renewed from day to day. Then life shall be kept ever fresh; then we shall go on from strength to strength, and thus bear much fruit that the Father may be glorified.

If all this be true, we need to know the Holy Spirit aright. As the Third Person, it is His office and work to bring the life of God to us, to hide himself in the depth of our being and make himself one with us, to reveal the Father and the Son, to be the mighty power of God working in us, and to take control of our entire being. He asks but one thing: simple obedience to His leading. The truly yielded soul will find in the daily renewing of the Holy Spirit the secret of growth and strength and joy.

CHAPTER TWENTY-SEVEN

The Daily Renewal—The Pattern

"Seeing that ye have . . . put on the new man, which is renewed in knowledge after the image of him that created him" (Col. 3:9, 10).

"If so be that ye have heard him, and have been taught by him . . . be renewed in the spirit of your mind; and that ye put on the new man, which after God is created in righteousness and true holiness" (Eph. 4:21, 23, 24).

In every pursuit, it is important to have the goal clearly defined. It is not enough that there be movement and progress; we want to know whether the movement is in the right direction. Especially when we are working in partnership with another, on whom we are dependent, we need to know that our aim and his are in perfect accord. If our daily renewal is to attain its object, we need to know clearly and hold firmly to what its purpose is.

"Ye have . . . put on the new man, which is renewed in knowledge." The divine life, the work of the Holy Spirit within us, is no blind force, as in nature. We are to be workers *together* with God; our co-operation is to be intelligent and voluntary—the new man is being renewed day by day "in knowledge." There is no knowledge which the natural understanding can draw from the Word, but which is without the life and the power, the real truth and substance, which the spiritual knowledge brings. The renewing of the Holy Spirit gives the true knowledge, which does not consist in thought and conception, but in an inward tasting, a living reception of the things of which the words and thoughts are but the images. "The new man which is renewed in knowledge." However diligent our Bible study may be, there is no true knowledge gained beyond the spiritual renewal that is being experienced; only the renewal "in the spirit of your mind," in its life and inward being, brings true divine knowledge.

What revelation of spiritual knowledge should be sought as the renewal's true and only aim? The new man "is being renewed in knowledge after the image of him that created him." *Nothing less than the image, the likeness of God.* That is the one aim of the Holy Spirit in His daily renewing; that must be the aim of the believer who seeks that renewing.

This was God's purpose in creation: "Let us make man in our image, after our likeness." How little the infinite glory of these words is considered! For nothing less than this did God breathe His own life into man that it might reproduce in man on earth a perfect likeness to God in heaven. In Christ, that image of God has been revealed and seen in human form. We have been predestined and redeemed and called, we are being taught and shaped by the Holy Spirit, to be conformed to the image of the Holy Spirit, to be conformed to the image of the Son, to be imitators of God, and to walk even as Christ walked. How can daily renewal be carried on, what can daily Bible study and prayer profit unless we set our heart on what God has set His on: the new man being renewed day by day "after the image of him that created him"?

In the second passage, the same thought is expressed somewhat differently. "Be renewed in the spirit of your mind; and . . . put on the new man, which after God [according to the likeness of God] is created in righteousness and true holiness." Righteousness is God's hatred of sin and preservation of the right. Holiness is God's indescribable glory—this perfect harmony of righteousness and love, His infinite exaltation above the creature, perfect union with man. Righteousness in man includes all God's will for our duty to Him and our fellowmen; holiness includes our personal relation to himself. As the new man has been created, so it daily must be renewed, "in righteousness and true holiness." To secure this, the power of the Holy Ghost works in us, and He waits for us day by day to yield ourselves to Him, in His renewing grace and power.

The morning hour is the time to secure the Holy Spirit's daily renewal into the image of God as righteousness and true holiness. We need meditation and prayer to set the heart upon what God is aiming at, and get a true vision of the wondrous possibility: the inward man renewed daily into the very likeness of God, changed into the same image by the Spirit of the Lord. Christian! let nothing less be your aim, or satisfy your aspirations. The image of God, the life of God in you, His likeness can be seen in you. No longer separate God and His likeness; approach Him and trust Him, with no other desire than to find Him in His likeness formed into you by the renewing of the Holy Spirit.

Let this be your daily prayer, to be renewed after the image of Him who created you.

CHAPTER TWENTY-EIGHT

The Daily Renewal—Its Cost

"For which cause we faint not; but though our outward man perish, yet the inward man is renewed day by day" (2 Cor. 4:16).

"Be not conformed to this world: but be ye transformed by the renewing of your mind" (Rom. 12:2).

It is not a small or an easy thing to be a full-grown, strong Christian. On God's side, it means that it cost the Son of God His life; it needs the mighty power of God to re-create a man; and only the unceasing daily care of the Holy Spirit can maintain that life.

From man's side it demands that when the new man is put on, the old man be put off. All the dispositions, habits, pleasures, of our own nature, that make up the life in which we have lived, are to be put away. All we have by our birth from Adam is to be sold if we are to possess the pearl of great price. If a man is to follow Christ, he must deny himself and take up his cross, to forsake all and follow Christ in the path in which He walked. He is to cast away not only all sin, but everything, however needful, legitimate or precious, that may become the occasion of sin; he is to pluck out the eye or cut off the hand. He is to hate his own life, to lose it, if he is to live in "the power of an endless life." To be a true Christian is a far more serious thing than most people think.

This is especially true of the daily renewing of the inward man. Paul speaks of it as being accompanied and conditioned by the "perishing" of the outward man. The whole epistle (2 Corinthians) shows us how the fellowship of the sufferings of Christ, including conformity to His death, was the secret of his life in power and blessing to the churches. "Always bearing about in the body the dying of the Lord Jesus, that the life also of Jesus might be manifested in our body. For we which live are always delivered unto death for Jesus' sake, that the life also of Jesus may be made manifest in our mortal flesh. So then death worketh in us, but life in you" (2 Cor. 4:10-12). The full experience of the life in Christ in our person, our body, our work for others, depends upon our fellowship in His suffering and death. There can be no large measure of the renewal of the inward man without the sacrifice, the death of the outward.

To be filled with heaven, the life must be emptied of earth. We have the same truth in our second text, "Be ye transformed by the renewing of your mind." An old house may be renewed, and yet keep very much of its old appearance; or the renewal may be so entire that men are amazed at the transformation. The renewing of the mind by the Holy Spirit means an *entire* transformation, an entirely different way of thinking, judging, deciding. The fleshly mind gives place to a "spiritual understanding" (Col. 1:9; 1 John 5:20). This transformation is not obtained except at the cost of giving up all that is of nature. "Be not conformed to this world, but be ye transformed." By nature we are of this world. When renewed by grace we are *still in the world,* subject to the subtle, all-pervading influence from which we cannot withdraw ourselves. Also, the world is *still in us* as the leaven of the nature which nothing can purge out but the mighty power of the Holy Spirit filling us with the life of heaven.

Let us allow these truths to take deep hold and master us. The divine transformation, the daily renewing of our mind into the image of Him who is from above, can proceed only as fast and as far as we have sought to be freed from every vestige of conformity to this world. The negative, "Be not conformed to this world," needs to be emphasized as strongly as the positive, "Be ye transformed." The spirit of this world and the Spirit of God contend for the possession of our being. Only as the former is perceived, renounced and cast out can the heavenly Spirit enter in and do His blessed work of renewing and transforming. The whole world and whatever is of the worldly spirit must be given up. The whole life and whatever is of self must be lost. This daily renewal of the inward man costs much as long as we are hesitating, or trying to do it in our own strength. Once we really learn that the Holy Spirit does all, and we by faith in the strength of the Lord Jesus have given up all, the renewing becomes the simple, natural, healthy, joyous growth of the heavenly life in us.

The inner chamber then becomes the place for which we long daily to praise God for what He has done, and is doing, and what we know He will do. Day by day, we yield ourselves afresh to the blessed Lord who has said, "He that believeth on me . . . out of his belly shall flow rivers of living water." The renewing of the Holy Spirit becomes one of the most blessed truths of our daily Christian life.

CHAPTER TWENTY-NINE

Holiness—The Chief Aim of Bible Study

"Sanctify them through thy truth: thy word is truth"
(John 17:17).

In His great intercessory prayer our Lord spoke of the
words which the Father had given Him, of His giving them
to His disciples, and of their having received and believed
them. This had made them disciples. Their keeping those
words would enable them to live the life and do the work of
true disciples. *Receiving the words of God from Christ, and
keeping them, is the mark and power of true discipleship.*

In praying the Father to keep them in the world when
He left it, our Lord asks that He would sanctify them in the
truth—His Word. Christ had said of himself, "I am the
truth." He was the "only begotten of the Father, full of
grace and truth." His teaching was not like that of the law
which came by Moses, giving a knowledge, a promise of
good things to come; this was but an image or a shadow.
"The words that I speak unto you, they are spirit, and they
are life" (John 6:63), giving the very substance and power
and divine possession of what they speak of. Christ spoke of
the "Spirit of truth" who would lead into all the truth that
there was in himself, not as a matter of knowledge or doctrine, but actual experience and enjoyment. Then He prays
that the Father would sanctify them in this living truth, as
it dwells in the Word and is revealed in Him by the Spirit.

"For their sakes," He says, "I sanctify myself, that they also might be sanctified through the truth" (John 17:19). And He asks the Father in His power and love to take charge of them, that His objective—to sanctify them in the truth through His Word, which is truth—may be realized; that they, like himself, may be sanctified in truth. Let us study the wonderful lessons given here in regard to God's Word.

"Sanctify them through thy truth: thy word is truth." *The great object of God's Word is to make us holy.* No diligence or success in Bible study will really profit us unless it makes us humbler, holier men. In all our use of Holy Scripture this must be our main object. The reason there is often so much Bible reading with so little real result in a Christlike character is that "salvation through sanctification of the Spirit and belief of the truth" (2 Thess. 2:13) is not truly sought. People imagine that if they study the Word and accept its truths, this will in some way, of itself, benefit them. But experience teaches that it does not. The fruit of holy character, of consecrated life, of power to bless others, does not come for the simple and most natural reason—that we only get what we seek. Christ gave us God's Word to make us holy; only when we make this our definite aim in all Bible study will the truth (not the doctrinal truth, but its divine quickening power, imparting the very life of God that it contains as a seed) open and impart itself to us.

"Sanctify them through thy truth: thy word is truth." Only God himself can make us holy by His Word. The Word, separate from God and His direct operation, cannot avail. The Word is an instrument; God himself must use it. God is *the* Holy One. He alone can make holy. The unspeakable value of God's Word is that it is God's means of holiness. The terrible mistake of many is that they forget that God alone can use it or make it effective. It is not enough that I have access to the dispensary of a physician. I need him to prescribe. Without him my use of his medicines might be fatal. So it was with the scribes. They made their boast of God's law; they delighted in their study of Scripture and yet remained unsanctified. The Word did not sanctify them because they did not seek for this in the Word, and did not allow God to do it for them.

"Sanctify them through thy truth: thy word is truth." Holiness through the Word must be sought and waited for from God in prayer. Our Lord taught His disciples that they must be holy; He also sanctified himself for them that they might be sanctified in truth; but most importantly, He brought His words and His work to the Father with the prayer that He would sanctify them. It is necessary to know God's Word and meditate on it. It is necessary to set our heart upon being holy as our first and chief objective in studying the Word. But all this is not enough; everything depends upon our following Christ in asking the Father to sanctify us through the Word.

It is God, the Holy Father, who makes us holy by the Spirit of holiness who dwells in us. He works in us the very mind and disposition of Christ who is our sanctification. "There is none holy but the Lord"; all holiness is His, including what He gives by His holy presence. The tabernacle and temple were not holy by virtue of cleansing, or separation or consecration. They became holy by the indwelling God. His taking possession made them holy. Even so God makes us holy as His Word brings Christ and the Holy Spirit into us. The Father cannot do this unless we tarry quietly before Him, and in deep dependence and full surrender give ourselves up to Him. It is in the prayer offered in the name, and the fellowship, and the faith of the Great Intercessor— "Sanctify me through thy truth: thy word is truth," that the Father's sanctifying power is found, and our knowledge of God's Word truly makes us holy.

The morning watch is sacred. It is the hour specially devoted to the soul's yielding itself up to God's holiness, to be sanctified through the Word. Let us always remember that the one aim of God's Word is to *make us holy*. Let it be our continual prayer, "Father, sanctify me through thy truth."

CHAPTER THIRTY

Psalm 119 and Its Teaching

"O how love I thy law! it is my meditation all the day.
Consider how I love thy precepts! My soul hath kept thy
testimonies; and I love them exceedingly" (Ps. 119: 97,
159, 167).

One portion of Holy Scripture is wholly devoted to
teaching us the place which God's Word ought to have in
our esteem and the way we can secure its blessing. It is the
longest chapter in the Bible, and, with hardly an exception,
in every one of its 176 verses mention is made of the Word
under different names. Anyone who really wants to know
how to study his Bible according to God's will ought to
make a careful study of this Psalm. There ought to come a
time in his life when he resolves to study its teaching and
carry it out into practice. How can we wonder that our Bible study does not bring more spiritual profit and strength
if we neglect the "Divine Directory" it provides us for that
study. Possibly you have never read it once through as a
whole. If you have not time, find time, some free Sabbath
hour (or why not some free weekday hour?) in which you
read it through and try to take in its chief thought, or at
least to catch its spirit. If you find it difficult to do this by
reading it once, read it more than once. This will make you
feel the need of giving it more careful thought. The following hints may help you to study this Psalm:

1. Note all the different names by which God's Word is
spoken of.

2. Note all the different verbs expressing what we ought to feel and do in regard to the Word. Then consider carefully what place God's Word claims in your heart and life, and how every faculty of your being—desire, love, joy, trust, obedience, action is influenced by it.

3. Count and note how many times the writer speaks in the past tense of his having kept, observed, adhered to or delighted in God's testimonies; how many times he expresses in the present tense how he rejoices in, loves, and esteems God's law; and how, in the future tense, he promises and vows to observe God's precepts to the end. Total these and see how more than a hundred times he presents his soul before God as one who honors and keeps His law. Study this especially (for these expressions are connected with his prayers to God) until you have a clear image of the righteous man whose fervent, effectual prayer "availeth much."

4. Study the prayers themselves and note the different requests he makes with regard to the Word, whether for the teaching to understand and the power to observe it, or for the blessing promised in the Word, and to be found in doing it. Note especially prayers like "Teach me thy statutes," or "Give me understanding." Also those where the plea is, "according to thy word."

5. Count the verses in which there is any allusion to affliction, whether from his own state, or his enemies, or the sins of the wicked, or God delaying to help him; and learn why it is in the time of trouble that we need God's Word especially, and that this alone can bring comfort to us.

6. Here is one of the most important things. Mark how often the pronouns thou, thine, thee occur, and how often they are used in petition, "Teach thou me," "Quicken thou me." You will see how the whole psalm is a prayer spoken to God. All the Psalmist has to say about the Word of God, whether with regard to his own attachment to it, or his need of God's teaching and quickening, is spoken upwards into

the face of God. He believes that it is pleasing to God and good for his own soul to connect his meditation and thoughts on the Word as continually and as closely as possible, by prayer, with the living God himself. Every thought of God's Word instead of drawing him off from God leads him to fellowship with God.

The Word of God becomes to him the rich and inexhaustible material for holding communion with the God whose it is and to whom it is meant to lead. As we gradually get an insight into these truths, we shall get a new meaning from the single verses. And when, from time to time, we take a whole paragraph with its eight verses, we shall find how they help to lift us up, with and through the Word, into God's presence and into that life of obedience and joy which says "I have sworn, and I will perform it, that I will keep thy righteous judgments" (Ps. 119:106). "O how love I thy law! it is my meditation all the day."

Begin to seek, by the grace of the Holy Spirit, to have the devotional life which this Psalm reveals integrated into your morning watch. Let God's Word every day, and before everything else, lead you to God. Let every blessing in it be a matter of prayer, especially your need of divine teaching. Let your intense devotion to it be your childlike plea and confidence that the Father will help you. Let your prayers be followed by the vow that as God quickens and blesses you, you shall run the way of His commandments. Vow to let all that God's Word brings you make you the more earnest in longing to carry that Word to others, whether for the awakening or the strengthening of the life of God in the soul.

CHAPTER THIRTY-ONE

The Holy Trinity

"For this cause I bow my knees unto the Father . . . that he would grant you . . . to be strengthened with might by his Spirit in the inner man; that Christ may dwell in your hearts through faith; that ye, being rooted and grounded in love, may be able to . . . know the love of Christ, which passeth knowledge, that ye might be filled with all the fulness of God. Now unto him that is able to do exceeding abundantly above all that we ask or think, according to the power that worketh in us [the Holy Spirit], unto him be glory . . . by Christ Jesus throughout all ages. . ." (Eph. 3:14, 16-21).

This passage has often, and with good reason, been regarded as one of the highest expressions of what the life of a believer may be on earth. And yet this view is not without its dangers; it may foster the idea that such an experience is to be regarded as something exceptional and distant, and hide the blessed truth that, in varying degree, it is meant to be the certain and immediate heritage of every child of God. Each morning each believer has the right and the need to say, "My Father will strengthen me today with power and is strengthening me even now, in the inner man through His Spirit." Each day we are to be content with nothing less than the indwelling of Christ by faith, a life rooted in love and made strong to know the love of Christ. Each day we believe that the work of being filled with all the fullness of God is being carried on and accomplished in us. Each day we ought to be strong in the faith of God's power, and be giving Him glory in Christ, for He is able to do above what we ask and think, according to the power of the Spirit working in us.

The words are, among many other things, remarkable for the way in which they present the truth of the Holy Trinity in its bearing on our practical life. Many Christians understand that it is right and needful at different times, in the pursuit of the Christian life, to give special attention to the three persons of the Trinity. However, they often feel it difficult to combine the various truths into one, and to know how to worship the Three in One. Our text reveals the wonderful relationship and the perfect unity. The Spirit is within us as the power of God, and yet He does not work at our will or His own. It is the Father who, according to the riches of His glory, grants us to be strengthened "by his Spirit in the inner man." It is the Father who does "exceeding abundantly above all that we ask or think, according to the power that worketh in us." The presence of the Spirit within us renders us more absolutely and unceasingly dependent on the Father. The Spirit can work only as the Father works through Him. We need to combine the two truths—a deep, reverent, trustful consciousness of the indwelling Holy Spirit, with a continual and dependent waiting on the Father to work through Him.

Even so with Christ. We bow our knees to God as Father in the name of the Son. We ask Him to strengthen us through the Spirit for one purpose: that Christ may dwell in our heart. So the Son leads to the Father and the Father again reveals the Son in us. As the Son dwells in the heart, and the heart is rooted and grounded in love, drawing its life out of divine love as its soil, producing fruit and doing works of love, we are consequently filled with all the fullness of God. The whole heart, with the inner and outer life, becomes the scene of the blessed interchange of the operation of the Trinity. As our hearts believe this we give glory, through Christ, to Him who is able to do more than we can think by His Holy Spirit.

What a wonderful salvation takes place in our heart: the Father breathing His Spirit into us, and by His daily renewing fitting us to be the home of Christ; the Holy Spirit ever revealing and forming Christ within us, so that His very nature, disposition and character become ours; the Son imparting His life of love, and leading us on to be filled with all the fullness of God.

This is meant to be our everyday religion. Let us worship the Three-One God in the fullness of faith every day! In whatever direction our Bible study and prayer lead us, let this ever be the center from which we go out and to which we return. We were created in the image of the Three-One God. The salvation by which God restores us is an inward salvation; it is worthless to us if it is not accomplished in our heart and enjoyed there. The God who saves us can do it in no other way than as the indwelling God, filling us with all His fullness. Let us worship and wait; let us believe and give Him glory.

Have you ever noticed in Ephesians how the three persons of the Trinity are continually mentioned together?

1:3. The Father, Jesus Christ, spiritual (Holy Spirit) blessings.

1:12, 13. To the praise of His Glory, the Father, in Christ, sealed with the Holy Spirit.

1:17. The Father, our Lord Jesus, the spirit of wisdom.

2:18. Access through Christ, in one Spirit, to the Father.

2:22. In Christ, a habitation of God, through the Spirit.

3:4-9. The mystery of Christ, hid in God, preached by the grace of God, revealed by the Spirit.

4:4-6. One Spirit, one Lord, one God and Father.

5:18-20. Filled with the Spirit, giving thanks to God, in the name of Christ.

6:10-18. Strong in the Lord, the whole armor of God, the sword of the Spirit, praying in the Spirit.

As you study and compare these passages, and seek to gain some true and humble conception of the glory of our God, notice especially how intensely practical this truth of the Holy Trinity is. Scripture teaches little of its mystery in the divine nature; almost all it has to say has reference to God's work in us, and our faith and experience of His salvation.

A true faith in the Trinity will make us strong, bright, God-possessed Christians. The divine Spirit uniting himself with our life and inner being; the blessed Son dwelling in us, effecting perfect fellowship with God; the Father, through the Spirit and the Son working out His purpose—that we be filled with all the fullness of God.

Let us bow our knees unto the Father! Then the mystery of the Trinity will be known and experienced.

CHAPTER THIRTY-TWO

In Christ

"Abide in me, and I in you" (John 15:4).

All instruction proceeds from the outward to the inward. When some knowledge has been obtained of the literal, in words or deeds, in nature or history, the mind is prepared to seek for the inner meaning hidden in them. It is the same with the teaching of Scripture concerning Jesus Christ. He is presented as a man among us, before us, above us, doing a work for us here on earth, continuing that work for us still in heaven. Many Christians never advance beyond this concept: an eternal, exalted Lord in whom they trust for what He has done and is doing for them and in them. They know and enjoy so little of the power of the true mystery of Christ in us, of His inward presence, as an indwelling Savior.

The former and simpler view is that of the first three Gospels; the latter marks the Gospel of John. The former is the aspect of truth presented in the scriptural doctrine of justification. The latter is the teaching concerning the union of the believer with Christ and his continual abiding; this is especially taught in John and the epistles to the Ephesians and Colossians.

To Christians, who all ought to be preparing to carry Christ to their fellowmen, I say earnestly, let this abiding in Christ and Christ in you be not only a truth you hold in its right place in your scheme of Gospel doctrine. Rather, as a matter of life and experience, let it animate all your faith in Christ and fellowship with God. To be in a room means to have all that is in it at your disposal—its furniture, its comforts, its light, its air, its shelter. To be in Christ, to abide in Christ, is not a matter of intellectual faith or conception, but of spiritual reality.

Consider who and what Christ is. Consider Him in the five aspects that mark and reveal His nature and work. He is *the Incarnate One*, in whom we see how God's Omnipotence united perfectly the divine and human nature. Living in Him, we are partaking of the divine nature and of eternal life.

He is *the Obedient One*, living a life of entire surrender to God and perfect dependence on Him. Living in Him our life becomes one of complete subjection to God's will and continual waiting upon His guidance.

He is *the Crucified One*, who died for sin and to sin that He might take it away. Living in Him we are free from its curse and dominion; we live, like Him, in death to the world and our own will.

He is *the Risen One*, who lives forevermore. Living in Him, we share His resurrection power, and walk in newness of life, a life that has triumphed over sin and death.

He is *the Exalted One*, sitting on the throne and carrying on His work for the salvation of men. Living in Him, His love possesses us, and we give ourselves to Him to use in winning the world back to God.

Being in Christ, abiding in Him, means that the soul is placed by God himself in the midst of this wonderful environment of the life of Christ. This life is human and divine, utterly given up to God, in obedience and sacrifice, wholly filled with God in resurrection life and glory. The nature and character of Jesus Christ—His dispositions and affections, His power and glory—are the elements in which we live, the air we breathe, the life by which our life exists and grows.

The full manifestation of God and His saving love can come only by indwelling. In virtue of Christ's divinity and divine power, He can, to the extent that we abide in Him, dwell in us. To the extent that the heart with its love is given to Him in faith, and the will is in active obedience, He comes and dwells in us. We can say, because we know, "Christ liveth in me."

If this life, Christ in us and we in Him, is to be our real everyday life, its spirit must be renewed and strengthened through personal communion with God in the morning watch. Our access to God, our sacrifice to God, our expectation from God, must all be in Christ, in the living fellowship with Him. If you feel that you want to get nearer to God, to realize His presence, or power, or love, or will, or working, more fully; if you want to have more of God, come to God *in Christ*. Consider how He drew nigh to the Father in deep humility and dependence, in full surrender and entire obedience; then come in His spirit and disposition, in union with Him. Seek to take the very place before God that Christ has taken in Heaven, that of an accomplished redemption, of a perfect victory, of full access to God's glory. Take the very place before God that Christ took on earth on His way to victory and glory. Believe in His indwelling and enabling power in you; be confident of being accepted, not according to your attainment, but according to the genuineness of your heart's surrender and the completeness of your acceptance in Christ. Then you will be led on in the path in which Christ living in you and speaking in you will be truth and power.

CHAPTER THIRTY-THREE

Himself Alone

"When Jesus therefore perceived that they would come and take him by force, to make him a king, he departed again into a mountain himself alone" (John 6:15).

The Gospels frequently tell us of Christ's going into solitude for prayer. Luke mentions His praying eleven times. Mark tells us in his very first chapter, that after an evening when all the city had come to see Him, and He had healed many, "in the morning, rising up a great while before day, he went out, and departed into a solitary place, and there prayed" (Mark 1:35). Before He chose His twelve apostles, "he went out into a mountain to pray, and continued all night in prayer to God" (Luke 6:12). This thought of complete privacy appears to have deeply impressed the disciples, giving rise to John's significant expression, "He departed into a mountain himself alone," and Matthew also had written, "He went up into a mountain apart to pray: and when the even was come, he was there alone" (Matt. 14:23). The man Christ Jesus felt the need of perfect solitude. Let us humbly seek to find out what this means.

1. *Himself alone.* Entirely by himself, alone with himself. We know how much interaction with men draws us away from ourselves and exhausts our strength. The man Christ Jesus knew this, too, and felt the need of coming to himself again, of gathering all His powers, of renewing the consciousness of what He was and what He needed, in order

to fully realize His high destiny, His human weakness, His entire dependence on the Father.

How much more does the child of God need this. Whether it be amid the distraction of secular activities or religious service, whether it be for the maintenance of our own Christian life, or the renewal of our power to influence men for God, there is an urgent call to every believer to follow in his Master's steps, and find the place and the time where he can be with himself alone.

2. *Himself alone, with spiritual realities.* It is in the entire withdrawal from contact with the things that are visible and temporal that we are free to yield ourselves fully to the powers of the invisible world, and can allow them to master us. Jesus needed time and quiet regularly to realize the power of the kingdom of darkness which He had come to contend with and to conquer, the need of this world of mankind which He had come to save, the presence and the power of the Father whose will He had come to do. Nothing is more indispensable in Christian service. A person should at times set himself to think intensely on the spiritual realities with which as a matter of knowledge he is so familiar, but which often exercise so little power on his heart and life. The truths of eternity have an infinite power; they often seem powerless because we do not give them the time to reveal themselves. Himself alone—this is the only cure.

3. *Himself alone, with God the Father.* It is sometimes said that work is worship, that service is fellowship. If ever there were a man who could have dispensed with special times for solitude and fellowship, it was our blessed Lord. But He could not do His work or maintain His fellowship in full power without His quiet time. He felt the need as man of bringing all His work, past and future, and putting it before the Father, of renewing His sense of absolute dependence on the Father's power, and absolute confidence in the Father's love, in periods of special fellowship. When He said, "The Son can do nothing of himself," He was express-

ing the simple truth of His relation to God; it was this that
made His solitude a necessity and an unspeakable joy.

Would that every servant of God understood and prac-
ticed this blessed art, and that the Church knew how to
train its children into some sense of this high and holy privilege; every believer may and must have his time when he is
indeed alone with God. Oh, to have God all alone to myself,
and to know that God has me all alone to himself!

4. *Himself alone, with the Word.* As man our Lord had
to learn God's Word as a child; during the long years of His
life in Nazareth, He fed on that Word and made it His own.
In His solitude He discussed with the Father all that that
Word spoke of Him, and all the will of God it revealed for
Him to do.

In the life of the Christian, one of the deepest lessons
that he has to learn is that the Word without the living God
avails little; that the blessing of the Word comes when it
brings us to the living God; that the Word that we get from
the mouth of God brings the power to understand it and to
obey it. Let us learn the lesson; personal fellowship with
God in secret can make the Word to be life and power.

5. *Himself alone, in prayer.* Prayer allows a man to lay
open his whole life to God, and to ask for His teaching and
His strength. Just try for a moment to think what prayer
meant to Jesus; it was adoring worship, humble love, childlike pleading for all He needed. As little as we can understand this properly, can we realize what blessedness awaits
the man who knows how to follow in Christ's steps? He will
prove what great things God can do for one who makes this
his chief joy—to be with Him, himself alone.

Himself alone. The words open up to us the secret of the
life of Christ on earth, and of the life that He now lives in
us. One of the greatest blessings of His life in us by the Holy
Spirit is that He reveals and imparts to us all that the Word
means—himself alone.

CHAPTER THIRTY-FOUR

Soul-winning

"He that winneth souls is wise" (Prov. 11:30).

In an article in *The Student Movement* entitled, "A Spiritual Awakening," I found the following sentences: "In the constitutions of most Students' Christian Unions it is stated that *the chief aim* of the S.C. Union is to lead students to become disciples of Jesus Christ. But if the question be pressed home, 'Are students actually being won from indifference and unbelief to faith in Jesus Christ?' the reply must be that, although in a few instances such is the case, in the majority of Unions it is very doubtful. Some Unions, discouraged by previous failure, have become skeptical as to the possibility of winning men for Christ in circumstances so difficult as their own. They may carry on to some extent traditional methods of aggressive work, but have ceased to expect to do more than strengthen such as already have faith. The leaders of the General College Department have definitely set the spiritual awakening of students in the forefront of their policy. If the local Unions will rally round the leaders, we may fully expect to see God working in the lives of those round about us. The love that won us can win many. It is right to recognize the seriousness of adopting this aim. It involves close companionship with Jesus Christ in holy living, in self-sacrifice, in loving service; it requires submission to the correction and control of God's Spirit. . . . We must lift the aim of winning students for Christ out of the background in our work and place it first. Our Unions have more than sufficient mechanical workers. They need men and women with definite aims, who will think and pray, and pray and work, until their Union is a fit instrument in God's hand for transforming the lives of students."

In an editorial in the same issue, I read with regard to a day of prayer: "There are many confessions, and many requests which we shall have to make on the day of prayer; but for ourselves we feel that the most urgent must be prayer for a spiritual awakening. We have been gradually recognizing the fact that the majority of our Unions are not winning men for Christ, and some have begun to realize with dismay that the fact has caused them very little sorrow. 'It is a misfortune certainly that students have not been won, but—what can we do?' Truly a spiritual awakening is needed; needed in our own hearts. When it comes, we shall soon find out what to do. Where is the passionate longing to help men? Where is the urgent prayer for our brother that will not be denied? At the very heart of the whole matter is our lack of interest. It is only what interests us that will influence men. It is only when deep down among the eternal interests of our soul there flames the passionate desire to lead men to Christ that we shall meet those who need our help, and who will welcome it. It is only words and deeds which burst from the burning passion of desire to help men, which find opportunities of influencing lives. For it is only where there is a desire like this that the Holy Ghost is a fellow worker with men. And without Him we are powerless, either to find those who are needy, or, having found them, to give them help. Shall we not unitedly ask that a passion for souls may be born in each of us on the day of prayer?"

To this let me add an extract from an article on "Indian Needs" in another issue of the same paper. The writer had spoken of the central purpose in the creation of Mission

Colleges being "the personal influence which the teachers would be able to gain over their pupils." He had then said: "Yet I have it on the authority of teachers in four of the largest Indian Mission Colleges that their time is so fully taken up with lecturing that they have neither time nor spirit for personal fellowship with their students. Five or six hours a day, with several more in preparation, in an Indian climate leave a man exhausted, with neither time nor energy for that intensest of all work, individual dealing with a man about his soul."

He concludes his paper with these words: "40,000 men are wanted, not less, if all India is to hear. Yet one almost shrinks from an appeal for men. Why? Lest men should come to be cumberers of the ground. For missionary work is, after all, only soul-winning. And there is nothing to make a man a soul-winner in India who has not been one at home. A sense of duty, or of the great need, may bring a man to India. Nothing can enable him to live year by year a missionary life out here, save such a burning love for Christ as constrains to sacrifice and a life of soul-winning at home."

What thoughts these excerpts suggest in regard to the work of soul-winning! It is the first great requisite in the missionary. Going to a mission field will not necessarily make a man a soul-winner. It is at home, before one enters the mission field, that the spirit of self-sacrifice and soul-winning must be gained and be exercised. Training its members in the art of soul-winning is one of the chief aims of the student movement, as the practice of it will be the measure of its strength and success. The danger continually threatens of our lapsing out of this into traditional and mechanical methods. Continual, fervent, united and private prayer ought to be made for more love to souls, and continual, earnest, united and private efforts be put forth in every Students' Union that our companions may be won for Christ.

The great characteristic of the divine life, whether in God, or in Christ, or in us, is *love seeking to save the lost.* Let this be the Christian life we cultivate: a love that finds its happiness in saving men. This life can be cultivated only by close personal attachment to Jesus and daily fellowship with Him as a friend we love. It is in the inner chamber that this fellowship with the Father and the Son is to be maintained. Here the Father who sees us in secret will reward us openly.

CHAPTER THIRTY-FIVE

The Power of Intercession

"Tell me . . . wherein thy great strength lieth." This is the question we would have asked of men who, as intercessors for others, have had power with God and have prevailed. More than one, who has desired to give himself to this ministry, has wondered why it was so difficult to rejoice in it, to persevere, and to prevail. Let us study the lives of the leaders and heroes of the prayer world; maybe some of the secrets of their success will be revealed to us.

The true intercessor is a man who knows that his heart and life are wholly given up to God and His glory. This is the only condition on which an officer at the court of an earthly ruler could expect to exert much influence. Moses and Elijah and Daniel and Paul prove that it is so in the spiritual world.

Our Lord himself proves it. He did not save us by intercession but by self-sacrifice. His power of intercession is established in His sacrifice; it claims and receives what the sacrifice won. This is clearly stated in Isaiah 53:12: "He hath poured out his soul unto death; and he was numbered with the transgressors; and he bare the sins of many, and *made intercession* for the transgressors." He first gave himself up to the will of God. There He won the power to influence and guide that will. He gave himself for sinners in all-consuming love, and so He won the power to intercede for them.

There is no other path for us. The man who seeks to enter personally into death with Christ, and gives himself wholly for God and men, will dare to be bold like Moses or

Elijah and will persevere like Daniel or Paul. Wholehearted devotion and obedience to God are the first marks of an intercessor.

You complain that you do not feel able to pray thus, and ask how you may be fitted to do so. You speak much of the feebleness of your faith in God, and love of souls, and delight in prayer. The man who is to have power in intercession must cease these complaints; he must know that *he has a nature perfectly adapted to the work.* An apple tree is only expected to bear apples, because it has the apple nature within it. "We are his workmanship, created in Christ Jesus unto good works" (Eph. 2:10). The eye was created to see; how beautifully suited it is for its work! You are created in Christ to pray; it is your very nature as a child of God.

The Spirit has been sent into your heart to do what? To cry "Abba Father," to lift your heart up in childlike prayer. The Holy Spirit prays in us with groanings that cannot be uttered, with a divine power which our mind and feelings cannot understand. Learn, if you would be an intercessor, to give the Holy Spirit much greater honor than is generally done. Believe that He is praying within you, and then be strong and of good courage. As you pray, be still before God to believe and yield to this wonderful power of prayer within you.

"But," you say, "there is so much conscious sinfulness and defect in our prayer." True, but have you not learned to pray *in the name of Christ*? Does the name not mean the living power? You are in Christ and He in you. Your whole life is hid and bound up in His, and His whole life is hid and working in you. The man who is to intercede in power must be very clear that, not only in thought and reckoning, but in actual, living, divine reality, Christ and he are one in the work of intercession. He appears before God clothed with the name and the nature, the righteousness and worthiness, the image and spirit and life of Christ. Do not spend the majority of your time in prayer in reiterating your petition, but in humbly, quietly, confidently claiming your place in Christ—your perfect union with Him, your access to God in

Him. It is the man who comes to God in Christ—as his life and his law and only trust—bringing to the Father that Christ in whom He delights, who will have power to intercede.

Intercession is supremely a work of faith—not a faith that tries only to believe that prayer will be heard, but a faith that is at home amid heavenly realities; a faith that does not trouble about one's own nothingness and feebleness, because it is living in Christ; a faith that does not make its hope depend upon feelings, but upon the faithfulness of the Three-One God; a faith that has overcome the world, and sacrifices the visible to be wholly free for the spiritual and heavenly and eternal to take possession of it; a faith that knows that it is heard and receives what it asks, and therefore quietly and deliberately perseveres in its supplication till the answer comes. The true intercessor must be a man of faith.

The intercessor must be a messenger—one who keeps himself ready, who earnestly offers himself personally to receive the answer and to dispense it. Praying and working go together. Think of Moses; his boldness in pleading with God for the people was no greater than his pleading with the people for God. We see the same in Elijah; the urgency of his prayer in secret was equalled by his jealousy for God in public, as he witnessed against the sin of the nation. Let intercession be always accompanied not so much by more diligent work as by meek and humble waiting on God to receive His grace and spirit, and to know more definitely what and how He would have us work. It is a great thing to take up the work of intercession—the drawing down to earth of the blessings which heaven has for one's every need. It is a greater thing as intercessor personally to receive that blessing, and go out from God's face, knowing that we have secured something that we can impart. May God make us all wholehearted, believing, blessing-bearing intercessors.

CHAPTER THIRTY-SIX

The Intercessor

"The effectual fervent prayer of a righteous man availeth much. Elias was a man subject to like passions as we are. . . " (James 5:16, 17).

Nothing so greatly weakens the impact of the call to imitate the example of Scripture saints as the thought that theirs are exceptional cases, and that what we see in them is not to be expected of all. The aim of God in Scripture is the very opposite. He gives us these men for our instruction and encouragement, as specimens of what His grace can do, as living expressions of what His will and our nature demand and render possible.

It was to meet this common error, and to give confidence to all of us who aim at a life of effective prayer, that James wrote, "Elias was a man subject to like passions as we are." Since there is no difference between his nature and ours, or between the grace that worked in him and works in us, there is no reason why we should not, like him, pray effectively. If our prayer is to have power, we must seek to have something of Elijah's spirit. The aspiration "Let me seek grace to pray like Elijah" is perfectly legitimate and most needful. If we honestly seek for the secret of his power in prayer, the path in which he walked will open to us. We shall find the secret in his life with God, his work for God, his trust in God.

1. *Elijah lived with God.*

Prayer is the expression of our life. As a man lives, so he prays. The bent of his heart as seen in his desires and actions, not the words or thoughts with which he is occupied at set times of prayer, is regarded by God as his real prayer. The life speaks louder and truer than the lips. To pray well I must live well. He who seeks to live with God will learn to know His mind and to please Him, and thus be able to pray according to His will. Consider how Elijah, at his first message to Ahab, spoke of "the Lord God, before whom I stand." Consider his solitude at the brook Cherith, receiving his bread from God through the ravens, and then at Zarephath through the ministry of a poor widow. He walked with God, he learned to know God well; when the time came, he could pray to a God whom he had proved. Only out of a life of true fellowship with God can the prayer of faith be born. Let the link between the life and the prayer be clear and close. As we give ourselves to walk with God, we shall learn to pray.

2. *Elijah worked for God.*

He went where God sent him. He did what God commanded him. He stood up for God and His service. He witnessed against the people and their sin. All who heard him could say, "I know that thou art a man of God, and that the word of the Lord in thy mouth is truth." His prayers were all in connection with his work for God. He was equally a man of action and a man of prayer. When he prayed down, first the drought and then the rain, it was, as part of his prophetic work, so that the people, by judgment and mercy, might be brought back to God. When he prayed down fire from heaven on the sacrifice, it was so that God might be known as the true God. All he asked was for the glory of God. How often believers seek power in prayer that they may be able to get good gifts for themselves. The secret selfishness robs them of the power and the answer. Only when self is lost in the desire for God's glory, and our life is devoted to work for God, can power to pray come. God lives to love, and save, and bless men; the believer who gives himself up to God's service in this will find new life in prayer. Work for others proves the honesty of our prayer for them. Work for God reveals both our need and our right to pray boldly. Cultivate the consciousness, and speak it out before God, that you are wholly given up to His service; it will strengthen your confidence that He is hearing you.

3. Elijah trusted in God.

He had learned to trust Him for his personal needs in the time of famine; he dared trust God for greater things in answer to prayer for his people. We see confidence in God's hearing him in his appeal to the God that answers by fire. We see confidence in God's doing what he would ask when he announced to Ahab the abundance of rain that was coming, and then, with his face to the earth, pleaded for it, while his servant six times brought the message, "There is nothing." An unwavering confidence in the promise and character of God and God's friendship, acquired in personal fellowship and proved in work for God, gave Elijah power for effective prayer.

The inner chamber is the place where this has to be learned. The morning watch is the training school where we are to exercise the grace that can prepare us to pray like Elijah. Let us not fear. The God of Elijah still lives; the spirit that was in him dwells in us. Cease from the limited and selfish views of prayer, which only aim at grace enough to keep us standing. Cultivate the consciousness that Elijah had, of living wholly for God, and we shall learn to pray like him. Prayer will bring to ourselves and to others the new and blessed experience that our prayers, too, are effective and avail much.

In the power of our Redeeming Intercessor, who ever lives to pray, let us take courage and not fear. We have given ourselves to God; we are working for Him. We are learning to know and trust Him. We can depend on the life of God in us, the Holy Spirit dwelling in us, to lead us on to this grace—the effectual prayer of the righteous man that availeth much.